RTI Is a Verb

To my wife, Ingrid, who makes it possible for me to learn and grow through support, encouragement, understanding, and love; and to our ever-growing brood of grandchildren—Isabella, Leah, Liam, and Kaiden. You make the pursuit of excellence in education all the more important.

—Tom Hierck

To Jill

—Chris Weber

RTI Is a Verb

Tom Hierck

Chris Weber

CORWIN
A SAGE Company

CORWIN
A SAGE Company

FOR INFORMATION:

Corwin

A SAGE Company

2455 Teller Road

Thousand Oaks, California 91320

(800) 233-9936

www.corwin.com

SAGE Publications Ltd.

1 Oliver's Yard

55 City Road

London EC1Y 1SP

United Kingdom

SAGE Publications India Pvt. Ltd.

B 1/I 1 Mohan Cooperative Industrial Area

Mathura Road, New Delhi 110 044

India

SAGE Publications Asia-Pacific Pte. Ltd.

3 Church Street

#10-04 Samsung Hub

Singapore 049483

Printed in the United States of America

Library of Congress Cataloging-in-Publication Data

A catalog record of this book is available from the Library of Congress.

ISBN: 978-1-4833-0748-0

This book is printed on acid-free paper.

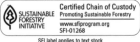

Acquisitions Editor: Jessica Allan

Associate Editor: Kimberly Greenberg

Editorial Assistant: Cesar Reyes

Production Editor: Melanie Birdsall

Copy Editor: Alison Hope

Typesetter: C&M Digitals (P) Ltd.

Proofreader: Annie Lubinsky

Indexer: Molly Hall

Cover Designer: Anupama Krishnan

13 14 15 16 17 10 9 8 7 6 5 4 3 2 1

Contents

About the Authors

Tom Hierck has been an educator since 1983 in a career that has spanned all grade levels and many roles in public education. His experiences as a teacher, an administrator, a district leader, a department of education project leader, and an executive director have provided a unique context for his education philosophy.

Tom is a compelling presenter, infusing his message of hope with strategies culled from the real world. He understands that educators face unprecedented challenges and knows which strategies will best serve learning communities. Tom has presented to schools and districts across North America with a message of celebration for educators seeking to make a difference in the lives of students. His dynamic presentations explore the importance of positive learning environments and the role of assessment to improve student learning. His belief that every student is a success story waiting to be told has led him to work with teachers and administrators to create positive school cultures and build effective relationships that facilitate learning for all students.

Tom Hierck's blog can be found at tomhierck.com/blog.

A native of Southern California, **Chris Weber, EdD,** has been in service to community and country his entire life. A graduate of the U.S. Air Force Academy, Chris flew C-141s during his military career. A former high school, middle school, and elementary school teacher and administrator, Chris has had a great deal of success helping students who historically underachieve learn at extraordinarily high levels.

As a principal and assistant superintendent in California and Chicago, Illinois, Chris and his colleagues have developed systems of response to intervention (RTI) that have led to heretofore unrealized levels of learning at schools across the country.

Chris is the best-selling author of *Pyramid Response to Intervention: RtI, PLCs, and How to Respond When Students Don't Learn; Pyramid of Behavior Interventions: 7 Keys to a Positive Learning Environment; Simplifying Response to Intervention: Four Essential Guiding Principles;* and *RTI in the Early Grades: Intervention Strategies for Mathematics, Literacy, Behavior, and Fine-Motor*

Challenges. These books have sold more than one hundred thousand copies worldwide. In addition, Chris's article in *Educational Leadership*, "The Why Behind RTI," was the most viewed article on the publication's website in 2010.

Chris is recognized as an expert in behavior, mathematics, and RTI. He consults and presents nationally to audiences on important educational topics, including Change and RTI—Preparing for Productive Teams; Behavioral RTI; Assessments for Tiers 2 and 3; If It's Predictable, It's Preventable—RTI in the Early Grades; Scheduling, Communication, and Coordination of RTI Schoolwide Teams; The *What* and *Why* of RTI; Evidence-Based Reading Strategies and Programs; and Common Core Mathematics—A Balanced Approach to Depth and Mastery.

In addition to writing and consulting on educational topics, Chris continues to serve in schools, working with teachers and students every day in Chicago, Illinois, at some of the highest-performing urban schools in the nation.

Acknowledgments

As you read through this book and find yourself inspired to add more to your toolbox, know that many hands helped to shape the final product. From the initial support of Kristin Anderson and Jessica Allan, to the insightful feedback from the editorial team of Alison Hope, Kimberly Greenberg, and Melanie Birdsall, to the marketing support from Stephanie Trkay, we've been in very good hands at Corwin. Having the opportunity to work and write together has been an amazing learning experience and added immensely to our roles as educators. Finally, a book goes through many iterations before becoming the product you are currently holding. In an effort to make this as practical and effective tool as possible we relied on the support of colleagues. Thanks to Greg Wolcott, Leeann Michalak Bartee, and Amy Mims for being "critical friends" and helping to shape the work.

1

Introduction
and the Research

Throughout this book, we will provide concrete recommendations and resources to allow educators to translate response to intervention (RTI) from research to practice, from ideas to reality. We will also connect the practices of RTI to decades of empirically validated research and best practice. But first, it's essential that we address the "Why?" questions: Why do we need to address changes to a system that has worked for the majority? Why is it important or necessary to reshape the last great bastion of a bygone era—the public school? Why are we looking to alter the notion of schools as the sorter of human potential and capacity? Invariably, the response to the "Why?" is because we know more about teaching and learning, we live in a world that is changing in significant ways; the opportunities that existed even a generation ago for students who did not graduate, or did not graduate with the skills essential for postsecondary opportunities or a skilled career, are almost nonexistent today. Once upon a time, schools served the purpose of imparting the academic requirements that were needed by the citizenry to function in their daily lives. Everything else that was required to function as a responsible member of the community was delivered at home by the immediate and extended family. While schools today are still charged with the responsibility of delivering the academic goods, they are also charged with the increased burden of delivering the social and emotional care that was once the purview of the home.

The world of work has also changed. In the United States, approximately seven thousand students drop out every school day (U.S. Department of Education, 2010). In bygone days this may not have been a significant factor, as a high school dropout with minimal skills could earn a living wage. This era has ended in the United States. In the 21st century, dropping out of school significantly diminishes the chances of securing a good job and a promising future. This is compounded even further when one considers the substantial financial and social costs to the communities, states, and countries in which dropouts live. Over the course of a lifetime, a high school dropout earns, on average, $260,000 less than a high school graduate (Alliance for Excellent Education, 2008). Dropouts from the class of 2010 alone will cost the United States more than $337 billion in lost wages over the course of their lifetimes (Alliance for Excellent Education, 2008). The discrepancy grows at an increased rate when comparing dropouts to those who complete a college or university degree. Recent statistics in British Columbia, Canada, indicate that an adult with a postsecondary degree will make $879,300 more than dropouts over the course of a career. Finally, advances in technology have rendered the view of the teacher as the only source of knowledge as a relic of schools we once knew. Knowledge acquisition is the easy part for today's learners; their various devices rapidly gather information that once took hours or days to uncover. Students today are connected to more people and knowledge, in ways unknown a generation ago. Using knowledge, critiquing points of view, and synthesizing information is the new expectation for students . . . and teachers.

The demands on the school system of today are significant, and the expectations for graduates greater. These expectations apply to all students: students who respond immediately to core instruction as well as students who will require additional time and differentiated support. Buffum, Mattos, and Weber (2011) clarify that all students include "any student who will be expected to live as a financially independent adult someday" (p. 24). Requiring that all students graduate with the ability to enter a postsecondary institution or a skilled career with the 21st century skills required to continue to learn further heightens the challenge. The statistics above support that notion wholeheartedly. RTI, then, is about so much more than interventions. It defines what we are as a profession and philosophically underpins the reflective checkpoints we use to assess the extent to which all students are learning.

As schools and districts refine and redefine their values, we would be wise to examine the practices and research that have endured for decades. The work of Ron Edmonds (1979) and Larry Lezotte (1991) and the Effective Schools Movement; Benjamin Bloom (1968, 1984) and Tom Guskey (2007) and Mastery Learning; and Grant Wiggins and Jay McTighe (2005) and Understanding by Design (UbD) provide the connections that ground the tenets of RTI and allow them to flourish.

EFFECTIVE SCHOOLS MOVEMENT

The birth of the Effective Schools Movement arguably marked the beginning of education as a modern profession, and continues to define the moral imperative of teaching and learning. Founders Ron Edmonds and Larry Lezotte outlined the seven correlates of effective schools as follows.

1. Safe and Orderly Environment

Schools are orderly, purposeful, and businesslike, free from the threat of physical harm. The school climate is not oppressive; it's conducive to teaching and learning. However, a safe and orderly environment does not simply involve the absence of undesirable student behavior. A school environment conducive to learning for all necessitates an increased emphasis on desirable behaviors involving students taking active responsibility for their learning and working in collaborative partnerships. To accomplish these goals, adults in schools must model collaborative behaviors in professional relationships. Teachers must learn the *technologies* of teamwork and schools must create the opportunities for collaboration. Staff must nurture the belief that collaboration will lead to higher levels of student learning and working environments that are more professionally satisfying. Students will work together cooperatively when they learn to respect human diversity and appreciate democratic values, and when they have the opportunity to interact with the 21st century skills that will prepare them for postsecondary opportunities or a skilled career. RTI is built on the tenets of creating a positive learning environment for all students. Tier 1 supports for all students, with progressively more intensive interventions in response to student needs as appropriate, lead to a positive learning environment for all. Educators gain information about each individual student and gain the capacity to respond with appropriate strategies to ensure all students learn at high levels.

2. Climate of High Expectations for Success

School staff must believe, and demonstrate the belief, that *all* students can attain mastery of essential school skills, and staff must also believe that they have the capability to help all students achieve that mastery. Expectations cannot simply describe the attitudes and beliefs of teachers within the teaching-learning situation, such as the even distribution of questions among all students and the equal opportunity for all students to participate in the learning process. Teachers will find themselves in the difficult position of starting with high expectations, and acting on them, and yet finding that some students have not yet learned. Teachers, teams, and schools must develop a broader array of responses. High expectations for success will be judged not only by initial staff beliefs and behaviors, but also by the school's response when some students do not learn. Schools must restructure time and resources to ensure that teachers have access to more *tools* to help them successfully achieve learning for all. Schools must be transformed from institutions designed for *teaching* to institutions designed to ensure *learning*. The instructional model used in the RTI framework has application to core academics *and* behavior, and is based on the notion of increasing the intensity of instruction based on student need. The value and strength of RTI lies in the provision of more-targeted, intensive, and explicit supports in response to student needs. Differences between tiers are characterized by significance of the student need and the intensity of the supports.

3. Instructional Leadership

In an effective school, the principal acts as an instructional leader and effectively, and with patient persistence, communicates the mission described above to staff, parents, and students. The principal understands and applies the characteristics of instructional effectiveness to the management of the instructional program. And yet instructional leadership cannot reside exclusively with the principal and administrative staff of the school. Instructional leadership must be broadened and leadership dispersed to all adults. The principal cannot be the only leader in a complex organization, but must create a community of shared values. The role of the principal must be as a leader of leaders, rather than a leader of followers. When building leaders and classroom teachers agree on the why of RTI, they work closely to ensure its cohesive and consistent implementation. The clarity of a written plan detailing steps of the implementation is essential as a road map to consistency. The principal, skilled as an instructional leader rather than as a school manager, establishes and maintains an RTI model as the first and most important job. Among other responsibilities, the school's leader makes decisions about staff, time, and material allocations to support the model.

4. Clear and Focused Mission

A clearly articulated school mission—in which the staff shares an understanding of and commitment to the instructional goals, priorities, assessment procedures, and accountability—is insufficient. Staff must accept responsibility for *all* students' *learning* essential skills and attributes. Schools must clearly define *all* and *learning*. *All* means all, including children of the poor, students with unique learning needs, and English learners. *Learning* must represent an appropriate balance between critical thinking and those more-basic skills prerequisite to higher-level learning. Students supported by a team of educators who collaborate for learning success are far more likely to succeed. This notion of collaboration is essential to successful RTI implementation and the outcome of this collaboration should guide decision making. The goal is to create and implement instructional and intervention strategies with a high probability of success. Successful implementation requires focused leadership and collaborative practices among all educators in a school and district. This clear and focused mission allows for RTI implementation to become a seamless schoolwide and districtwide model.

5. Opportunity to Learn and Student Time on Task

A significant, and increased, amount of classroom time must be allocated to instruction related to essential skills through well-planned learning activities. Teachers cannot be oriented toward covering content at a breakneck pace. Interdisciplinary curriculum and a clear, collaborative understanding of *essential* content is a must. Schools must courageously declare that some things are more important than others, be willing to abandon less-critical content to dedicate energy to those areas that are valued most, and adjust the available time that students spend on essentials so that they reach mastery. The use of research-based instructional practices at each tier is crucial to achieving outcomes. As a student moves through Tiers 2 and 3, educators may not involve other programs, but instead use the core curriculum with increased intensity. Focusing on achievement levels and setting goals for advanced students are also parts of the RTI approach, as is bringing struggling students to grade level, which is more widely but inaccurately understood as the sole focus of RTI.

6. Frequent Monitoring of Student Progress

Schools must measure student progress toward mastery frequently through a variety of assessments to improve individual student performance and the instructional program. The quantity of data, the requisite specificity of data, and the rate at which schools must respond to data will necessitate the use of technology. This same technology and these same assessments should also allow students to monitor their own learning and adjust their own behavior. Monitoring of student learning must also increasingly emphasize more authentic assessments of mastery, with less emphasis on multiple-choice tests. Increased attention must be paid to the alignment between the intended, taught, and tested curriculum. To effectively use data to drive decisions in the RTI model, educators must understand what data will be collected, how often staff and students will monitor progress toward mastery at different tiers, what instruments and materials will be used, and who will collect the data. Douglas B. Reeves (2009) suggests that schools and districts are drowning in data, but thirsty for evidence. We must consider the function of data as well as the source.

7. Home-School Relations

Parents must understand and support the school's basic mission and must be given the opportunity to play an important role in helping the school to achieve this mission. The relationship between parents and the school must be an authentic partnership. Schools must clearly identify the ways in which parents can be involved and must take an active role in ensuring parents comprehend the rules of school. In the RTI approach, parent involvement is characterized by meaningful two-way communication where parents are informed of intervention options for their children before they are implemented. At Tier 1, parent involvement in school decision making may lead to an improved, more-positive school climate. At the Tier 2 and 3 levels, when some portions of the intervention may extend to the home, parent expertise regarding the individual student is vital.

While the notion of Mastery Learning may have earlier roots, the subject really gained momentum in education as a result of the work of Benjamin Bloom (1968). Bloom looked at the approach taken by teachers to organize curriculum into instructional units and modified it to include two components that he believed would improve the results for students. Feedback and corrective procedures became the hallmark of Bloom's Mastery Learning. Rather than assessments being used to mark the end of units, Bloom suggested they be used in a formative fashion to identify areas of struggle for students (and by extension areas that may need adjustments in the instructional phase for teachers). Once identified, these struggles could be remedied through individualized, corrective procedures. These correctives would be specific to items from the assessment so as to provide clarity for the student and teacher. Following corrections, the student would receive a second, mirrored assessment that served two roles: it would verify the efficacy of the corrective action, and it would provide a motivational tool for the student. Bloom also suggested that additional enrichment activities ought to be considered for students who successfully master the unit content so as to broaden and expand their learning. We view Bloom's Mastery Learning as a forerunner to Tier 2 academic supports.

Guskey (2007) has furthered the work of Bloom and made a strong connection between Mastery Learning and RTI. In a 2011 paper with Jung, the two authors suggest that RTI and Mastery Learning represent powerful tools in schools' efforts to help all students learn at high levels. The commonalities between the two approaches are identified as follows.

MASTERY LEARNING

1. Universal Screening (RTI) and Diagnostic Pre-Assessment With Preteaching (Mastery Learning)

Both RTI and Mastery Learning involve a method of assessing students prior to beginning instruction. These quick diagnostics focus on knowledge, skills, and behaviors required for students to be successful in the upcoming unit. In both RTI and Mastery Learning, the intent is to identify which students might be at risk of learning difficulties based, in part, on whether the student possesses the entry-level skills needed to be successful in the unit.

2. High-Quality, Developmentally Appropriate Initial Instruction (Tier 1 in RTI and Group-Based Instruction in Mastery Learning)

Engagement of all students in high-quality instruction using evidence-supported teaching strategies is key to both approaches. This instruction should focus on essentials, be contextualized and differentiated, and include meaningful learning activities within the general education classroom for all students, regardless of current levels of readiness or label (e.g., special education, English learner).

3. Progress Monitoring (RTI) and Formative Assessment (Mastery Learning)

Regular and systematic monitoring of student results and progress is another common element of the two approaches. In RTI the intent of this monitoring is to determine if students are benefiting from instruction and intervention and, if not, to inform instruction and intervention that is more effective. The frequency of these checks varies depending on subject and class configuration. Mastery Learning includes regular formative assessments that are designed to check students' learning of the critical learning goals of the unit. These are followed by diagnostic feedback to students on their learning progress. Both types of formative assessment ultimately provide information to students to guide their learning and close any gaps.

4. Appropriate, Evidence-Based Intervention (Tier 2 in RTI and Corrective Instruction in Mastery Learning)

Both approaches anticipate that some students may still experience some learning challenges and need further assistance after initial instruction. The progress monitoring and formative assessments mentioned above provide the clarity that allows teachers to respond. Specialists or assistants may assist classroom teachers in providing intervention that is qualitatively different from the initial instruction. The key to this step is not *teaching slower and louder*, but rather using an alternative instructional approach and allocating more time.

5. Additional Progress Monitoring (RTI) and Second Formative Assessments (Mastery Learning)

The two approaches require frequent progress checks to ensure that students are learning and that interventions are working.

6. Specialized, Highly Intensive Instruction (Tier 3 in RTI)

Tier 3 in RTI represents supports that will be necessary for a small percentage of students. These students have been screened to be at risk for failure based on current information or have not responded adequately to less-intensive supports and likely lack knowledge for foundational prerequisite skills. Schools will likely need to provide individual students intensive interventions to ameliorate significant deficits in foundational skills, as well as scaffold access to essential, core content. While Mastery Learning does not have a comparable step, Bloom did anticipate that some students might require individualized tutorial time that would target their specific learning needs.

7. Enrichment or Extension Activities (Mastery Learning)

Mastery Learning clearly identifies the need for additional extension activities for those students who can demonstrate mastery of unit concepts. Rather than a traditional approach of more of the same, Mastery Learning suggests providing activities that broaden the learning experiences of students. Within an RTI framework, students who master essential content presented in Tier 1 may pursue interesting, enriching activities rather than moving farther ahead of their peers who struggled with concepts, thereby allowing the teacher to maintain some capacity to plan out the learning progressions of the whole class.

UNDERSTANDING BY DESIGN

Developed by Grant Wiggins and Jay McTighe, Understanding by Design (UbD) is another framework for improving student achievement. UbD emphasizes the teacher's role as a designer of student learning with clearly defined learning targets, as a creator of assessments that are strong indicators of student understanding, and as a planner of engaging and effective lessons. UbD is based on several key ideas.

- A critical goal of education is the development and deepening of student understanding. Rather than a traditional approach of rote memorization focused on drill and kill, UbD aims to nurture students' genuine learning and deep conceptual understanding. When teachers provide students with the opportunity to explain, interpret, apply, shift perspective, empathize, and self-assess, they can better assess understanding.
- Effective curriculum development involves a three-stage process called backward design that clearly defines and describes student learning outcomes prior to initiating classroom activities. This process challenges the notion of the textbook as instructor, and prevents teaching from becoming activity orientated, both of which diminish the establishment of clear priorities and purpose. Wiggins and McTighe (2005) define the three stages as follows:
  - *Stage 1.* Identify desired results: enduring understandings, essential questions, and knowledge objectives.
  - *Stage 2.* Determine the types of evidence needed to assess and evaluate student achievement of the desired results.
  - *Stage 3.* Design learning activities that promote students' mastery of desired results and their subsequent success on assessment tasks.
- Student and school performance gains are achieved through regular reviews of results (achievement data and student work) followed by targeted interventions to curriculum and instruction. Teachers administer formative assessments, gather evidence from students, and gain feedback from colleagues, using that feedback to adjust instructional practices.
- Teachers, schools, and districts engage in collaborative efforts to design, share, and peer-review units of study.

UbD and RTI intersect in three key areas—identifying desired results, determining acceptable evidence, and planning learning experiences and instruction. UbD complements RTI by clearly defining the main purpose for doing the work; ensuring that learning targets are clear; and focusing on learning, not on teaching or testing. UbD also informs RTI by defining what the evidence of learning might look like, clarifying essential performance tasks, defining other sources of evidence, and identifying how success will be measured. Finally, UbD helps center RTI's focus on Tier 1 by identifying what we need to teach and in what order, what best practices exist, and what tools we might use to achieve our goals.

There are other important systems of educational practice that have been connected to RTI and that contribute to response to intervention, most notably those associated with professional learning communities. (While RTI is most commonly known as response to intervention in the educational literature, we encourage educators to interpret RTI as students' responses to both instruction and intervention.) RTI is a framework for organizing schools in which systems exist to guarantee that every student receives the time and support they need to be successful. RTI is not a fad, but builds on the foundations of the Effective Schools Movement, Mastery Learning, and UbD. RTI is a process for ensuring higher levels of academic and behavioral success for all students. Full and rigorous implementation of RTI requires schools to provide high-quality instruction, balanced assessment, and time for collaboration. RTI systems use a multitiered system of support to identify and respond to student needs, which will include and require authentic family involvement, data-based decision making, and effective leadership at both the school and district levels. While RTI has entered into schools' consciousness and practices as a result of the Individuals with Disabilities Education Act (IDEA), due in part to the superiority of RTI over the discrepancy model as a way of determining the presence of a learning disability for the purposes of eligibility for special education services, it is most useful as a representation of the cultures and structures required to meet the needs of all learners.

RTI is simply a framework that helps define the time and support that all students need to be successful. In simple terms, RTI may best be understood as a verb: To what extent are students responding to instruction and intervention; that is, to what extent are they RTI'ing? When data and other evidence suggest that students are RTI'ing, then we continue to provide similar supports. When data and other evidence suggest that students are not responding to instruction, we begin a smooth process of determining what supplemental time and support (interventions) may be necessary to ensure that students begin responding as soon as possible.

RTI involves every staff member. Classroom teachers deliver and differentiate instruction. They assess to ensure students are mastering standards, help diagnose to determine specific areas of need, monitor student progress to ensure that supports are working, and communicate this information to other staff. Paraprofessionals and interventionists help provide supplemental supports to students in need and provide feedback regarding observations and assessments of student progress. Clinicians assist in diagnosing, problem solving, assessing, and providing direct supports to students in need. Administrators oversee the entire process and assist in all steps as necessary and hold all staff accountable for the consistent implementation of all processes, including regular team meetings, to check on the progress of students. Every educator's goal must be for every student to possess the academic and behavioral skills to be on track for postsecondary education or a skilled career. RTI is simply the best and most research-based, evidence-based framework for guiding us in ensuring that every single student meets that goal. John Hattie, for example, after his exhaustive meta-analysis of decades of educational practices across the globe, rates RTI as one of the top three ideas ever to be employed on behalf of students.

The culture and structures of RTI do not simply build on the powerful work of Ron Edmonds and Larry Lezotte, Benjamin Bloom and Tom Guskey, and Grant Wiggins and Jay McTighe; RTI helps us fulfill the promise and potential of our profession. High levels of learning for all is not simply our ethical responsibility to the students we serve; it's a practical necessity for students, our schools, and our nations.

SCHOOL CULTURE

At the conclusion of each chapter we will address the collective will required to accomplish the tasks discussed within the chapter and describe strategies to address these obstacles. In our experiences, the actual work required to implement RTI in schools, beginning with the foundational steps of identifying and unpacking essential standards, will not overwhelm staff or inhibit their success. Educators are more than professionally capable of completing this work. The obstacles that derail schools in their efforts are most often based on a lack of will. Here are a few cultural challenges that schools may face:

- **The system works for most kids so why change? Is it really possible to have *all* students succeed?**

Often the people with whom we work are successful products of a school system (with success being defined as completing a degree and working in the field of education), and so staff may question why change is needed. Similarly, many parents who willingly and frequently interact with the school are successful products of a bygone school system and they also wonder, "Why is change needed?" One of the biggest reasons for continuous improvement is that we know more today about teaching and learning than at any other point in the history of education. We can, and must, do better for many of the reasons outlined in the text above. Think about most other professions: Haven't they progressed over the previous decades? We need to incorporate the best of what we have learned today with the best of what we know worked yesterday to prepare our students for tomorrow.

As for the question of *all* students, we remain steadfast in the belief that not only is this desirable, but it also is achievable. Educators can and must learn from successful schools that face the challenges of poverty, immigration, race, single-parent households, schools that might despair but that still thrive rather than wither. This is not to suggest prescriptive replication of those schools but instead that we extract from these sites what works, contextualized to your location, to ensure all students succeed.

- **It's sink or swim in the real world, and that's the way it should be in our schools.**

While the former part of this statement may have some validity, the latter part misses the true reason for why schools exist. They are not factories where empty minds are filled to prepare the masses for the real world, but instead are learning institutions whose role is to ignite the passion of students so they can make valuable and valued contributions to the communities in which they will live. The role of the teacher is not to predict the future, but to create it. If the world is sink or swim, we need to prepare our students by teaching them how to swim.

- **My job is to teach and their job is to learn.**

This notion belies the fact that the learning is the teaching. The best measure of teacher efficacy is demonstrated learning by students. "Did they learn?" truly answers the question "Did I teach?" more effectively than simply relying on sound pedagogy. Hamre and Pianta's 2005 study of students identified as being at risk, cited in Daniel Goleman's *Social Intelligence: The New Science of Human Relationships* (2006) found that those placed with cold or controlling teachers struggled academically—regardless of whether their teachers followed pedagogic guidelines for good instruction. But if these students had a warm and responsive teacher, they flourished and learned as well as other kids. Our job is to create the conditions where learning is the best option available to our students.

The next six chapters will provide a comprehensive framework for describing how schools can put RTI into action, because interpreted most powerfully, RTI is a verb that will lead to high levels of learning for all.

Chapter 2. Content and Instruction in Tier 1. Focus instruction with high standards.

- Transform student engagement and achievement by creating high-impact classrooms.
- Develop common formative assessments (CFAs), and classroom assessments or tasks.
- Adopt and use next-generation standards, such as the Common Core State Standards (CCSS), with a local perspective.
- Support curriculum design by focusing all educators on clear (unpacked and unwrapped) essential priority standards.
- Improve assessment literacy to focus educators on specific student needs.
- Plan, implement, monitor, and model engaging, high-yield instructional strategy frameworks.
- Leverage professional development to ensure clear understanding of excellent teaching and learning.
- Determine when and how to use which strategies for which students.

Chapter 3. Common Formative Assessments, Evidence, Data Analysis, and Collaboration. Leverage teams as the vehicle for school improvement.

- Use data to monitor and improve teaching and leadership practices.
- Effectively use collaboration and data analysis consistently across the system.

- Ensure collaborative data analysis is driving instructional decision making.

Chapter 4. Information Within RTI: Screening, Progress Monitoring, and Diagnoses. Evidence is the engine that drives an RTI-based system of supports.

- Universal screening assessments identify students in immediate need of intensive, Tier 3 supports.
- Diagnoses help identify the causes of student difficulty.
- Progress monitoring tools help inform the extent to which students are responding to interventions.

Chapter 5. Tier 2 and 3 Interventions, Strategies, and Resources. Students with identified areas of need require our best alternative approaches.

- High-leverage reading supports.
- Timely, impactful writing interventions.
- Alternative, visual, and conceptual supports for mathematics.
- Simple, evidence-based strategies for improving behaviors.

Chapter 6. Social and Academic Behavioral Interventions. Behavior and academics are inextricably linked and our approach to both must be consistent.

- Simple, evidence-based strategies for improving social behaviors.
- Research-based methods of improving academic behaviors, those self-regulatory and executive functioning skills so essential to success in life and school.
- Resources for precorrecting and deescalating misbehaviors.

Chapter 7. Lead the Work With Confidence, Leadership, and Accountability. Create focused and supportive accountability so leaders and teachers make the best decisions.

- Lead and inspire the work.
- Ensure that the logistics—the structures—of RTI are comprehensively in place.
- Use key leadership research and intensive professional development to plan, implement, and monitor sustainable improvement.
- Create a clear and useful accountability system that is linked to adult actions in addition to test scores.

Classroom teachers, specialists, clinicians, special education staff, and district offices are hungry for specific guidance on RTI. RTI, while a potentially promising and positive guiding presence for schools, has often been misunderstood and misapplied. The following detailed description of RTI, with easy-to-use, sound templates, will support schools in reculturing and restructuring our efforts to ensure high levels of learning for all. When combined with professional development support on *how* to apply the thinking and templates within this book, and by ensuring that the thinking that guides the work validly and accurately represents both the *why* and *what* of RTI, we are confident that it can be a transformative resource for schools across the United States and Canada.

Content and Instruction in Tier 1

Systematic processes are absolutely essential to ensuring that all stakeholders are accountable and supported to ensure that RTI results in high levels of learning for all students. We'll begin with the core . . . with what we do with all students . . . with where we spend the majority of our time and energies: Tier 1.

KEY CORE CONTENT

RTI can perhaps best be understood as a *verb*. Collaborative teams of educators provide high-quality, differentiated instruction, and then analyze evidence of student learning. This evidence is the way in which educators determine the effectiveness of instruction. In analyzing evidence of learning, teams are asking, "Have students *responded* to *instruction?*" If it's predictable, it's preventable, and we can predict that some students will require additional time and supplemental, targeted supports to learn at high levels. Therefore, we must be prepared with the time, personnel, and resources to provide extra assistance. This extra assistance may be called an intervention. We frequently check on the progress of students receiving interventions; we collaboratively ask, "Have students *responded* to *intervention?*" RTI is a verb. It guides our work with students, whether that work is provided to all students (also known as Tier 1, or core instruction) or to some students (also known as Tiers 2 and 3, or supplemental intervention).

It all starts with carefully and completely defining key core content. Why must we define key core content?

- Learning, and the curriculum we determine is most essential for students to learn, will only be guaranteed and viable if teams of educators define it clearly (Marzano, 2001).
- There are too many standards, even in light of the CCSS initiative (DuFour & Marzano, 2011; Schmoker, 2011).
- Standards must be unpacked so that educators and students know what mastery looks like, so instruction can match these expectations, and so teams of educators can backwards plan (McTighe & Wiggins, 2005).
- The better our understanding of content and the more precisely we unpack and unwrap standards, the better our assessments of student learning. This will lead to more accurate identifications of students in need of extra support, more diagnostic analyses of specific areas of need, and more targeted interventions.
- We cannot expect to help all students achieve an appropriate depth and complexity of understanding with all standards; we must prioritize which standards are critical.
- We cannot intervene and provide more time and differentiated supports on all standards with students at risk; identifying the essential learning (prioritized standards) helps determine the focus of interventions.
- How do we systematically, carefully, and completely define key core content?
- We collaboratively prioritize which standards or learning targets are the most critical for all students to master. We use prioritized standards synonymously with essential, power, or critical standards.
- We collaboratively unpack standards so all teachers and students understand the level of rigor and format associated with mastery, as well as the types of learning that logically precede and follow mastery of the essentials.
- We collaboratively unwrap standards to ensure that we are assessing student mastery as accurately and authentically as possible. Not all learning can be assessed with a multiple-response test. We will misidentify students in need of extra assistance and miss opportunities to learn about the effectiveness of instruction if we do not more-accurately match assessment to the levels of understanding that we expect.

Thus, there are three steps to defining key core content: (1) prioritizing standards, (2) unpacking standards, and (3) unwrapping standards. The following sections and templates describe and provide examples of how educators can complete these steps, which are prerequisite and fundamental to our RTI efforts.

PRIORITIZING STANDARDS

As noted above, even next-generation standards such as the Common Core State Standards represent an overly broad set of learning targets for students to master at an appropriate level of depth and complexity. An agreed-on set of standards is critical to ensuring a guaranteed, viable curriculum, but "the sheer number of standards is the biggest impediment to implementing standards" (in Scherer, 2001, p. 15). Teams of teachers must prioritize standards. While there may be five standards represented in a unit of study, teams must identify which are *must-know* and which are *nice-to-know*. Predictably, this process is difficult for teams who are intimate with the content. It's a classic "can't see the forest for the trees" scenario. However, we have found there is one team of teachers that can definitely define the essential content for fourth-grade students to master: the fifth-grade teachers who will be assuming primary responsibility for fourth-grade students' learning in a year's time. Prioritizing standards is a must; the following templates and explanations can assist teams in collaboratively identifying the standards and learning targets that they should prioritize. The guiding questions are an extension of the work of Reeves (2002) and Ainsworth (2003a) and can be understood by reviewing the following steps (also see Table 2.1 on page 18):

1. List standards in the *Standard* column.

   Grade 4 Reading Standards: Foundational Skills (K–5):

   3. Know and apply grade-level phonics and word analysis skills in decoding words:

      a. Use combined knowledge of all letter-sound correspondences, syllabication patterns, and morphology (e.g., roots and affixes) to accurately read unfamiliar multisyllabic words in context and out of context (National Governors Association Center for Best Practices, & Council of Chief State School Officers, 2010a, p. 17).

2. If necessary and desired, list targets that better represent specific learning tasks in the *Learning Target* column:
   For example,

   Grade 4 Reading Standards: Foundational Skills (K–5):

   Know and apply all digraphs, diphthongs, and blends in decoding and making meaning

   Know and apply syllable patterns in decoding and making meaning

   Know and apply roots in decoding and making meaning

   Know and apply prefixes in decoding and making meaning

   Know and apply suffixes in decoding and making meaning

   Read unfamiliar multisyllabic words

3. Ask about the standard or learning target: "Is it a prerequisite for the next grade level?" That is, is this standard *specifically* needed to be successful in the next grade?
   If yes, write a 1. If no, write a 0.

4. Ask about the standard or learning target: "Is it important within other content areas?" This standard represents thinking that will directly contribute to success in other subject areas.

If yes, write a 1. If no, write a 0.

5. Ask about the standard or learning target: "Is it a critical life skill for college and career readiness?" This standard represents the types of thinking associated with 21st century skills.

If yes, write a 1. If no, write a 0.

6. Ask about the standard or learning target: "Is it heavily weighted on state tests?" This standard will be more heavily assessed on Smarter Balanced, Partnership for Assessment of Readiness for College and Careers, or related high-stakes assessments.

If yes, write a 1. If no, write a 0.

7. Ask about the standard or learning target: "Is it an area of need for your students?" Evidence, data, professional judgment, and/or experiences suggest that this standard represents an area of relative weakness for our students.

If yes, write a 1. If no, write a 0.

8. Total your responses in the five columns and use that sum to help prioritize standards. The number of prioritized standards will vary from school to school, but staff will be able to confidently state, "At the conclusion of this unit (or chapter or quarter or trimester or school year), all students will demonstrate mastery of these standards."

9. Using the six levels of Bloom's revised taxonomy, identify the level of this standard. Each level within the taxonomy represents skills worth knowing, but in our experience, levels 1–2 are overrepresented; ensure a balance exists.

Bloom's Revised Taxonomy:

6 *Creating.* Generating new ideas, products, or ways of viewing things (designing, constructing, planning, producing, inventing)

5 *Evaluating.* Justifying a decision or course of action (checking, hypothesizing, critiquing, experimenting, judging)

4 *Analyzing.* Breaking information into parts to explore understandings and relationships (comparing, organizing, deconstructing, interrogating, finding)

3 *Applying.* Using information in another familiar situation (implementing, carrying out, using, executing)

2 *Understanding.* Explaining ideas or concepts (interpreting, summarizing, paraphrasing, classifying, explaining)

1 *Remembering.* Recalling information (recognizing, listing, describing, retrieving, naming, finding)

Connection to RTI

The best intervention is prevention. When core, Tier 1 instruction focuses on depth over breadth, all students benefit. Students with lower levels of readiness will have time to receive preteaching and reteaching within the unit of instruction. Students currently on grade level engage with more depth and complexity when content is prioritized. Students with more well-developed current levels of readiness will have time to explore enriched aspects of the prioritized standards. More students respond to initial instruction. This applies to academic skills, just as it applies to social and academic behaviors.

10. Using the four levels of Webb's Depth of Knowledge (1997), identify the level of this standard. Again, each level represents skills worth knowing; ensure a balance exists. (See Table 2.1.)

4 *Extended Thinking.* Investigating, or applying to, real-world contexts; requiring time to research, think, and process multiple conditions of the problem or task; involving nonroutine manipulations across disciplines and content areas

3 *Strategic Thinking.* Reasoning with knowledge; developing a plan or sequencing steps to approach problem; requiring some decision making and justification, more abstract and complex, often more than one possible answer

2 *Basic Application of Skill/Concept.* Using information; developing conceptual knowledge, following or selecting appropriate procedures, with two or more steps and decision points along the way; solving routine problems; organizing and displaying data

1 *Recall.* Recalling or recognizing facts, information, concepts, or procedures

Teams should review and reflect on their determinations of prioritized standards regularly. Evidence of student learning and vertical articulation between grade levels and adjacent courses will lead to more-informed decisions on the most critical content for students to master.

Behavior and academics are inextricably linked. This is particularly true for students at risk (Buffum et al., 2009, 2010, 2011; Hierck, Coleman, & Weber, 2011; Weber, 2013). When students are not responding to core instruction in essential academic content, the causes of these difficulties may be deficits in basic academic needs—students may have deficits in literacy or numeracy that are compromising their ability to access content or demonstrate mastery. Alternatively, students who are not responding to core instruction in essential academic content may simply need more time and/or differentiated supports.

Table 2.1 Prioritizing Standards

Standard	Learning Target	Is it a prerequisite for the next grade level? (1 or 0)	Is it important within other content areas? (1 or 0)	Is it a critical life skill for college and career readiness? (1 or 0)	Is it heavily weighted on state tests? (1 or 0)	Is it an area of need for your students? (1 or 0)	Total	Bloom's Revised (1–6)	Webb's Depth of Knowledge (1–4)

Another possibility that we must consider is that students' misbehavior, either in the domain of social or academic behaviors (e.g., self-regulatory strategies or executive functioning skills), is inhibiting their success in mastering grade-level or content essentials. It is rare to find a student whose academic difficulties have not led to behavioral challenges; it is equally rare to find a student whose inappropriate behaviors do not significantly impede learning. We must accept responsibility for teaching students the social and academic behaviors that we want to see.

Academic behavior is the term that we use for a cognitive skill that is integral to success in school and life. The concept is not new, and we have not introduced the concept to schooling. Whether known as self-regulatory strategies or executive functioning skills, these concepts are part of 21st century skills and postsecondary and career readiness expectations. Academic behaviors guide *how* students meet expectations for student success, whereas academic content standards describe *what* they master.

Do we expect students to already know how to behave and how to *study* in schools and in classrooms without any guidance on our behalf? Who knows and can define the ways in which students should behave to be successful? Parents have been in school and they know how to raise their children, but abdicating the responsibility for school behavior to parents is unfair and unrealistic. School behavior is our domain and our responsibility. School teams can and should use a modified Prioritizing Standards template for social and academic behaviors to identify the social-emotional skills on which they should focus content, instruction, reinforcement, and intervention, as modeled in Tables 2.2 and 2.3.

Social behaviors are critical in their own right. For students to be productive 21st century citizens, social behaviors are key. Collaboration and cooperation, two of many behaviors that we would define as social, are prominently identified in the Partnership for 21st Century Skills documents. Social behaviors are also critical because of their interconnectedness with academics. Students with challenges in the social-behavior domain will have difficulties learning academic skills, both because their behaviors distract them from fully participating in classroom experiences and because their behaviors remove them from the classroom due to visits to the office and suspensions. Resources such as *Pyramid of Behavior Interventions* (Hierck, Coleman, & Weber, 2011), Responsive Classroom (Northeast Foundation for Children, 2013), and Positive Behavior Interventions and Supports (Sugai & Horner, 2002) can provide additional guidance on proactive behavioral systems; it starts with determining what social behaviors must be prioritized for a school.

While schools are increasingly demonstrating their recognition of the importance of social behaviors through schoolwide initiatives, they are less commonly focusing on academic behaviors, which are equally important. If students do not understand the so-called secrets of school or the attributes of successful learners, their ability to learn the essential academic skills of any given school year will be impacted and their abilities to become self-regulating, long-term learners will be at great risk. Table 2.4 provides a sample of prioritizing academic behaviors.

Table 2.2 Prioritizing Behavior Standards

Standard	Learning Target	Is it directly connected to mastery of prioritized academic skills? (1 or 0)	Is it an area of need for your students? (1 or 0)	Total	For what levels of Bloom's and/or Webb's Depth of Knowledge is the behavior required? (1–6)

Table 2.3 Prioritizing Behavior Standards—Sample: Social Behaviors

Standard	Learning Target	Is it directly connected to mastery of prioritized academic skills? (1 or 0)	Is it an area of need for your students? (1 or 0)	Total	For what levels of Bloom's and/or Webb's Depth of Knowledge is the behavior required? (1–6)
Cooperation (Disruption)	Interfering with learning environment so student and others are negatively impacted.				
Social Respect (Defiance)	Refusing to comply with expectations (not from lack of understanding).				
Physical Respect (Aggression)	Hurting, or invading space of, others.				
Verbal Respect (Inappropriate language)	Directing disrespectful and hurtful comments toward others.				
Attention (Inattention)	Being unable to focus on instruction.				
Self-Control (Impulsivity)	Being unable to control oneself physically and verbally.				
Attendance (Absences)	Being absent so frequently that absences negatively impact learning.				
Honesty (Lying/cheating)	Being untruthful so that it impacts relationships and learning.				
Property Respect (Property damage/ vandalism)	Destroying school items and/or others and compromising opportunity to learn.				
Empathy (Harassment/ bullying)	Being inconsiderate of others, leading to challenges to relationships and learning.				

Table 2.4 Prioritizing Behavior Standards—Sample: Academic Behaviors

Standard	Learning Target	Is it directly connected to mastery of prioritized academic skills? (1 or 0)	Is it an area of need for your students? (1 or 0)	Total	For what levels of Bloom's and/or Webb's Depth of Knowledge is the behavior required? (1–6)
Metacognitive practices	Knowledge and beliefs about thinking				
Self-concept	Seeing oneself as smart				
Self-monitoring	Ability to plan and prepare				
Engagement	Ability to maintain interest				
Strategy	Techniques for organization and memorization, including rehearsal and elaboration				
Volition	Efforts needed to stay motivated				
Emotional control	Techniques for regulating response to situations				

A guaranteed and viable curriculum is among the most important commitments a school can make to students; it represents a commitment that will, by itself, lead to significant increases in student learning as schools focus more on depth of mastery than on breadth of coverage. However, prioritizing standards to ensure viability is not enough. Schools must ensure that teachers share a deep level of understanding about what mastery of prioritized standards means. To reach this important consistency of expectations, schools must unpack prioritized standards. Before we describe unpacking, however, we will provide more detailed information on academic and social behaviors.

College and Career Readiness

Next-generation standards, such as the CCSS, have the expectation of post-secondary and career readiness for all. Postsecondary and career readiness includes proficiency with academic behaviors, with the executive functioning and self-regulatory strategies that successful learners use. When schools are examining their core practices and prioritizing the content that they expect all students to master, they would be wise to consider resources and guidance from experts and policy groups regarding postsecondary and career readiness and 21st century skills. For example, in *College and Career Ready: Helping All Students Succeed Beyond High School*, David Conley (2010) lists skills that all students must possess to be ready for college or a skilled career:

- Analyzing text and participating in analytical discussions
- Writing persuasively
- Drawing inferences and conclusions from text
- Interpreting conflicting information from different sources
- Supporting arguments with evidence
- Solving complex problems with no obvious answers

Complementing Conley's list of essential attributes are the skills needed for continued postsecondary learning as described by the Educational Policy Improvement Center (EPIC):

- Key cognitive strategies (Think)
- Key content knowledge (Know)
- Key transition knowledge and skills (Go)
- Key learning skills and techniques (Act)

We have organized a site needs assessment for 21st century learning to assist schools as they continue to meet the more-complex demands of today's workplace:

Core Subjects

Mastery of core subjects. Core subjects include

- English, reading, or language arts
- World languages
- Arts

- Mathematics
- Economics
- Science
- Geography
- History
- Government and civics

How is your school ensuring that all students master these core subjects?

In addition to these subjects, schools must promote understanding of content at much deeper levels by weaving 21st century themes into core subject literacies:

Global Awareness Literacy

- Using 21st Century Skills to address global issues
- Learning from and working collaboratively with individuals representing diverse cultures, religions, and lifestyles in a climate of mutual respect and open dialogue
- Understanding other nations and cultures, including the use of non-English languages

Financial, Economic, Business, and Entrepreneurial Literacy

- Knowing how to make appropriate personal economic choices
- Understanding the role of economy in society
- Using entrepreneurial skills to enhance productivity and career options

Civic Literacy

- Participating in civic life, staying informed, and understanding governmental processes
- Exercising the rights and obligations of citizenship at local, state, national and global levels
- Understanding the local and global implications of civic decisions.

Health Literacy

- Obtaining, interpreting, understanding, and using health information and services
- Understanding preventative physical and mental health measures
- Using information to make appropriate health-related decisions
- Establishing and monitoring personal and family health goals
- Understanding national and international public health and safety issues

Environmental Literacy

- Understanding the environment and the circumstances and conditions affecting it
- Understanding society's impact on the natural world
- Investigating and analyzing environmental issues, and drawing accurate conclusions about effective solutions
- Taking individual and collective action toward addressing environmental challenges

How is your school ensuring that all students master these literacies?

Learning and Innovation Skills

Learning and innovation skills are increasingly recognized as those that separate students who are prepared for an increasingly complex life and work environments in the 21st century and those who are not. A focus on creativity and innovation, critical thinking and problem solving, and communication and collaboration is essential to prepare students for the future.

Creativity and Innovation

- Thinking Creatively
  - Using a wide range of idea-creation techniques
  - Creating new and worthwhile ideas

o Elaborating, refining, analyzing, and evaluating ideas to improve and maximize creative effort

- Working Creatively With Others

  o Developing, implementing, and communicating new ideas effectively
  o Being open and responsive to new and diverse perspectives, and incorporating group input and feedback
  o Demonstrating originality and inventiveness and understanding the real world limits to adopting new ideas
  o Viewing failure as an opportunity to learn; understanding that creativity and innovation are long-term, cyclical processes

- Implementing Innovations

  o Acting on ideas to make tangible, useful contributions to the field

How is your school ensuring that all students master learning and innovation skills?

Critical Thinking and Problem Solving

- Reasoning Effectively

  o Using various types of reasoning (inductive, deductive, etc.)

- Using Systems Thinking

  o Analyzing how parts of a whole interact with each other to produce overall outcomes

- Making Judgments and Decisions

  o Analyzing and evaluating evidence, arguments, claims, and beliefs
  o Analyzing and evaluating major alternative points of view
  o Synthesizing and making connections between information and arguments

- o Interpreting information and drawing conclusions based on the best analysis
- o Reflecting critically on experiences

- Solving Problems

  - o Solving different kinds of nonfamiliar problems in both conventional and innovative ways
  - o Identifying and asking significant questions that clarify various points of view and lead to better solutions

How is your school ensuring that all students master critical thinking and problem solving?

Communication and Collaboration

- Communicating Clearly

  - o Articulating thoughts and ideas effectively using oral, written, and nonverbal skills
  - o Listening effectively to decipher meaning, knowledge, values, attitudes, and intentions
  - o Using communication for a range of purposes (e.g., to inform, instruct, motivate, and persuade)
  - o Using multiple technologies, predicting their effectiveness, and assessing their impact
  - o Communicating effectively in diverse environments (including multilingual environments)

- Collaborating With Others

  - o Demonstrating the ability to work effectively and respectfully in diverse teams
  - o Exercising flexibility and willingness to compromise to accomplish a common goal
  - o Assuming shared responsibility for collaborative work, and valuing the individual contributions made by team members

How is your school ensuring that all students master communication and collaboration?

Information, Media, and Technology Skills

Included in 21st century learning are three global givens: (1) access to an abundance of information, (2) rapid changes in technology, and (3) the ability to collaborate and contribute on an unprecedented scale. Effective citizens exhibit a range of skills related to information, media, and technology.

Information Literacy

- Accessing and Evaluating Information

    o Accessing information efficiently and effectively
    o Evaluating information critically and competently

- Using and Managing Information

    o Using information accurately and creatively
    o Managing the flow of information from a variety of sources
    o Understanding the ethical/legal issues surrounding the access and use of information

Media Literacy

- Analyze Media

    o Understanding both how and why media messages are constructed
    o Examining how messages are interpreted differently, how points of view are included or excluded, and how the media influence beliefs and behaviors
    o Understanding of the ethical/legal issues surrounding the access and use of the media

- Create Media Products

    o Using the most appropriate media-creation tools, characteristics, and conventions o Using the most appropriate expressions and interpretations in diverse, multicultural environments

Technology Literacy

- Applying Technology Effectively

  o Using technology as a tool to research, organize, evaluate, and communicate
  o Using digital technologies, networking tools, and social networks to access, manage, integrate, evaluate, and create information
  o Understanding the ethical/legal issues surrounding the access and use of information technologies

How is your school ensuring that all students master information, media, and technology skills?

Life and Career Skills

Life and work environments require more than thinking skills and content knowledge: the ability to navigate complex environments in the global age requires rigorous attention to developing life and career skills.

Flexibility and Adaptability

- Adapting to Change

  o Adapting to varied roles, job responsibilities, schedules, and contexts
  o Working effectively with ambiguity and changing priorities

- Being Flexible

  o Incorporating feedback effectively
  o Dealing positively with praise, setbacks, and criticism
  o Understanding, negotiating, and balancing diverse views and beliefs to reach workable solutions, particularly in multicultural environments

Initiative and Self-Direction

- Managing Goals and Time

  o Setting goals with tangible and intangible success criteria
  o Balancing short-term and long-term goals
  o Using time and managing workload efficiently

- Working Independently

  o Monitoring, defining, prioritizing, and completing tasks without direct supervision

- Self-Directing Learning

  o Going beyond basic mastery of skills to explore and expand learning
  o Demonstrating initiative to advance skill levels
  o Demonstrating commitment to learning as a lifelong process
  o Reflecting critically on past experiences to inform future progress

How is your school ensuring that all students master life and career skills?

Social and Cross-Cultural Skills

Interacting Effectively With Others

- Knowing when to listen and when to speak
- Conducting oneself in a respectful, professional manner

Working Effectively in Diverse Teams

- Respecting cultural differences and working effectively with people from a range of social and cultural backgrounds
- Responding with an open mind to different ideas and values
- Leveraging social and cultural differences to create new ideas and increase both innovation and quality of work

Productivity and Accountability

- Managing Projects
  - o Setting and meeting goals in the face of obstacles and competing pressures
  - o Prioritizing, planning, and managing work to achieve goals
- Producing Results
  - o Demonstrating attributes associated with high-quality productions, including

    Working positively and ethically

    Managing time and projects effectively

    Multitasking

    Participating actively, reliably, and punctually

    Presenting oneself professionally and with culturally sensitive etiquette

    Collaborating and cooperating effectively with teams

    Respecting and appreciating team diversity

    Being accountable for results

Leadership and Responsibility

- Guiding and Leading Others
  - o Using interpersonal and problem-solving skills to influence and guide others
  - o Leveraging strengths of others
  - o Inspiring others via modeling and selflessness
  - o Demonstrating integrity and ethical behavior
- Being Responsible to Others
  - o Acting responsibly with the interests of the larger community in mind

How is your school ensuring that all students master social and cross-cultural skills?

The point of sharing these postsecondary and career-readiness 21st century skills ideas is not to overwhelm staff already working at their limit: rather, the point is to further define the tasks that face schools and students, and to reinforce the importance of prioritizing content. If the thinking skills associated with postsecondary and career readiness and 21st century skills are to be mastered by all students, prioritizing standards is more important than ever.

Seven Keys to a Positive Learning Environment

We wrote *Pyramid of Behavior Interventions: Seven Keys to a Positive Learning Environment* (Hierck et al., 2011), for several reasons. We recognized then, as we recognize now, the inextricable link between academics and behavior. We observed that when systems of behavioral supports did not result in the success that schools sought, the cause was often a deficiency in one of the seven keys. Finally, we believed that to build and sustain a learning environment in which all students can learn at high levels, a systematic, well-defined process was necessary.

While we identify strategies and supports that may be appropriate as Tier 2 and 3 supports, the seven keys relate primarily to Tier 1:

1. Common expectations

    - Condense school rules, codes of conduct, and mission statements into a few easy-to-remember, positively phrased common words or phrases.
    - Link behavior expectations to academic expectations.
    - Ensure students, staff, and parents know the expectations.
    - Ensure everyone in the school uses this common language.
    - Ensure kids know the expectations.
    - Ensure adults model them.

2. Targeted instruction

    - All staff teaches schoolwide expectations directly to all students.
    - Give students opportunities to develop, practice, and demonstrate appropriate social skills.
    - Regularly review common expectations, practice them often, and recognize and reward them when students display them correctly.
    - Teach social skills and academic skills in the same way: demonstrate, practice, review, and celebrate.

3. Positive reinforcement

    - Catch kids being good. (Don't bribe.) Acknowledge.
    - Timely and specific feedback is critical to improved learning.
    - The words we use can be as, or more, powerful than any tangible reinforcer. Words should promote a growth mindset and positivity.
    - Reward the behavior, and not the student.
    - School staff members who are uncomfortable with tokens and rewards concentrate on recognizing students for displaying positive social and academic skills.

- Reinforce behaviors that we wish to see more commonly displayed intentionally and systemically (in the same manner, the same frequency, and for the same reasons).

4. Support strategies and interventions

- Staff analyzes the functions, causes, and antecedents of behavior.
- Staff agree on eight to ten evidence-based strategies to meet students' behavioral needs.
- Staff receive professional development and support on effectively using these strategies.
- Staff use strategies consistently.
- Staff use check in/check out (CICO) to mentor students and monitor their progress and the success of strategies.

5. Collaborative teams

- When a student's behavior escalates, a schoolwide team organizes supports.
- The team, with parent involvement, develops an individual plan specific to the needs of that child.
- Analyze observations and behavioral data.
- Plans are specific, observable, and measurable, and include consistent follow-up.
- Every staff member behaves collaboratively and cooperatively, and is willing to compromise to help all students in all situations.

6. Data-driven dialogue

- Systems for data collection are in place to track schoolwide behavior and academic progress.
- The quality and quantity of data may differ in order to better inform decision making.
- The information collected is specific enough to generate baseline data, trends, and patterns of behavior for individual students.
- Staff shares information in proactive ways to adjust, modify, reteach, and celebrate.

7. Schoolwide system approach

- Systems are in place to ensure that the pyramid of behavior interventions works consistently throughout the school.
- Students, staff, and parents know how the system works.
- Administrators model high expectations and devote time to—and place a priority on—social skills.
- The systems are secure enough to withstand staff changes, yet flexible enough to accommodate changes in situations and circumstances as they arise.

We believe that the seven keys to a positive learning environment provide schools with the guidance needed to build and sustain a schoolwide system of positive behavioral supports. Behavioral standards must receive the same attention as academic standards. Students are likely not responding to instruction and intervention due to difficulties with behavior, often because they are affected by academic challenges. We will describe additional assessments, interventions, and data-based processes in later chapters.

We are devoting a chapter of a book on RTI to content standards. Why should we examine, or reexamine, content in light of RTI?

• It's possible that a large percentage of students are deemed at risk simply because of the overwhelming quantity of content standards that we have attempted to teach, and that they have attempted to learn. Research from the Trends in International Math and Science Study (Gonzales, Williams, Jocelyn, Roey, Kastberg, & Brenwald, 2008) have repeatedly shown that the performance of U.S. students is average at best, and often below average, when compared to other industrialized nations. This remains true even when comparing the United States' highest performing states and most affluent students. A typical U.S. fourth-grade mathematics text totals 530 pages; a typical fourth-grade mathematics text in another industrialized country totals 170 pages (Hanushek, Peterson, & Woessmann, 2011). A typical U.S. fourth-grade science text totals 397 pages; a typical fourth-grade science text in another industrialized country totals 125 pages. The United States averages seventy-eight mathematics topics in a school, while Germany averages twenty-three and Japan seventeen. Students from both Germany and Japan significantly outperform U.S. students (Organisation for Economic Development and Co-Operation [OECD], 2011). While there are many notable differences between teaching and learning in the United States and higher performing nations, the sheer number of standards is undeniably vast (Ginsburg, Leinwand, Anstrom, & Pollock, 2005).

• There is no guarantee that those students who are currently meeting proficiency standards are on track to graduate ready for college or a skilled career. A Northwest Evaluation Association (NWEA; Cronin, Kingsbury, Dahlin, & Bowe, 2007) correlation of the tens of thousands of students nationwide found that students who met AYP on one large state's No Child Left Behind examination score at the twentieth percentile on NWEA assessments. A potential crisis may exist because a *separate* NWEA study (Cronin, Dahlin, Adkins, & Kingsbury, 2007) correlated college and career readiness closer to the sixty-fifth percentile. We may be communicating to teachers, students, and families that all is well, when in fact there is a large gap between meeting state and federal expectations and postsecondary and career readiness. A preponderance of evidence suggests that we must help students go deeper and solve more complex tasks. No teacher would conclude that this is possible with the current number of standards. We must focus.

UNPACKING STANDARDS

Teams must unpack standards so that staff build collective consensus on the rigor and format associated with mastery of grade-level standards. In addition, unpacking standards can inform differentiation; when teams describe in detail the quality of student work that will be required to demonstrate mastery of standards, they are in a great position to both identify necessary prerequisites and appropriate extensions. If it's predictable, it's preventable. We can predict that a few students will lack the prerequisite skills required to access new content. Let's be prepared by assessing which students lack which prerequisite knowledge, by planning time into our unit maps to provide this preteaching (an exceptional preventative support), and by identifying which staff members and which strategies would be the best match for these students' needs.

We can also predict that there will be students who can already demonstrate mastery of new content, or who will readily meet our expectations. Let's be prepared with tasks that authentically challenge students with activities of greater depth and complexity, instead of simply more work. The CCSS, for example, designed with coherence to allow for both access and acceleration, make the identification of prerequisite and enrichment skills and standards more clear (National Governors Association Center for Best Practices, & Council of Chief State School Officers, 2010a, 2010b).

The process of unpacking standards is both critical and time-consuming. Therefore, teams should begin by unpacking the standards that they have identified as priorities. This process directly impacts instruction and differentiation. When teachers understand the target that they are responsible for ensuring that students master, they can plan their instruction more precisely. This form of backward planning (Wiggins & McTighe, 2005) will ensure that first instruction is best instruction; that teams are in a position to provide preventative, proactive supports; that staff plan for Tier 1 supports and build them into core instruction; and that fewer students will require Tier 2 and 3 supports. The template and sample in Table 2.5 provide support to teams when unpacking standards.

As is the case with prioritizing standards, teams must also establish consistency on the details of social and academic behaviors. We can unpack these behaviors just as we unpack academic skills.

Unpacking standards ensures that teachers and students are crystal clear regarding the expectations of the prioritized standards. These unpacked standards drive instruction within a flexible unit. Ideally, prioritized and unpacked standards lead to fewer students at risk; educators must reject coverage of a breadth of all standards for a depth of mastery of prioritized standards. A thorough unpacking of standards also informs our first level of interventions in a system of RTI. Prerequisites and enrichment tasks that are directly related to prioritized standards are predefined for students with differing levels of readiness.

Another Thought on Standards. The standards movement has brought potential benefits and clarity to education, particularly in the possibility of describing a truly guaranteed and viable curriculum. The standards movement has also, perhaps inappropriately, segmented knowledge, yet different standards have so much in common. A brief examination of next-generation mathematics standards reveals remarkable commonalities between Number and Operations and

Table 2.5 Unpacking Standards

Standard	Standard in student-friendly, parent-friendly language	Evidence of mastery: What will it look like when students demonstrate mastery?	Prerequisites: What skills are required for students to access the essential standard?	Enrichment: How will students extend their mastery of the essential standard to greater levels of depth and complexity?

Connection to RTI

If it's predictable, it's preventable. We can predict that a few students will lack prerequisite skills required to access prioritized standards, putting them at risk before a new unit begins. We can predict that a few students will experience misunderstandings while engaging with prioritized standards within the unit. We can predict that a few students will demonstrate mastery of prioritized standards at the very beginning of the unit. Let's be prepared by collaboratively prioritizing and unpacking standards, and by building time into our flexible pacing guides to preteach, intervene, and enrich. Even with our improved and thoughtful efforts at improving core instruction, a few students will require intervention—more time and differential supports. Let's be ready.

Measurement and Data standards; Geometry standards share commonalities to Number and Fractions standards. Moreover, the close relationships of standards occur both between, and within, content. For example, the concept of cause and effect is fundamental to structures in literature and informational text, historical events in social studies, natural processes in science, and simple and complex equations in mathematics. The point is this: When you hear a colleague worry that we are not covering all the standards to be assessed on high-stakes tests, remember that we are not teaching isolated standards—we are teaching students to problem solve and think critically. These essential skills transcend standards.

UNWRAPPING STANDARDS

Standards, instruction, and assessment continuously interact. We should not be embarrassed by revealing that we often do not know where one ends and the other begins. As an example, the need to devote more time to prerequisite standards is informed through our instruction, when frequent checks for understanding, also known as informal assessments, reveal significant gaps in students' prior knowledge. The adjustments we make within flexible blocks of instruction help ensure a guaranteed, viable curriculum.

While standards, instruction, and assessments are interconnected and mutually informing, we have broken down the elements of great teaching in this chapter for the sake of clarity. We *prioritize* standards to guarantee the viability of our curriculum. We *unpack* standards to inform a consistently understood depth of instruction from which we can plan. We *unwrap* standards to inform the ways in which we must assess students and to determine the instruction that will prepare them for the task.

The reason is simple. The overwhelmingly dominant form of assessment in schools is selected response, and yet selected response tests are valid and accurate assessments for a fraction of the type of learning for which we want students to demonstrate mastery, and that we therefore measure. The four primary types of learning targets (Stiggins, 2007) are

- *Knowledge.* Involves mastery of substantive subject content that represents knowing and understanding. The most efficient (and quite accurate) method for assessing knowledge targets is a selected response format: matching, true/false, multiple choice.
- *Reasoning.* Involves using knowledge and understanding to draw conclusions and solve problems. The most appropriate method for assessing reasoning targets is an extended written response that requires students to fully describe their thinking.
- *Performance.* Involves the development of proficiency in completing a task where the *process* is as important as the product or outcome. Examples of assessing performance targets include playing a musical instrument, orally defending a position, reading aloud, speaking in a second language, or using a psychomotor skill.
- *Product.* Involves the ability to create tangible products that represent learning. Examples of assessing product targets include written work, science fair models, and art products, which meet certain standards of quality and that present concrete evidence of academic proficiency.

If we want students to reason, perform, and produce, we must design, administer, and analyze assessments that measure this type of learning. If we are going to assess in these ways, our instruction must prepare students for these tasks.

The rigor and format with which we assess must match the rigor and format implied by the prioritized standards. When unwrapping standards (Ainsworth, 2003b), we can

- UNDERLINE any *knowledge* targets—substantive subject content;
- BOX any *reasoning* targets—thinking skills;
- STAR any *performance skills*—processes students need to attain mastery of the standard; and
- Enclose in PARENTHESES any *products*—concrete, tangible evidence of learning.

The evidence that teacher teams notate while unwrapping can be inserted into the standard itself, or the evidence can be organized into a table such as Table 2.6.

Students may need to display their mastery of prioritized standards in a variety of ways because multiple learning targets are included in the standard. Teams must design and/or select assessments that match these types of targets.

The work of prioritizing, unpacking, and unwrapping standards may be more successful and efficient when educators use the tools in this chapter. This will positively impact student learning because it will be done collaboratively by teacher teams with the support of principals, district and site content area coaches, and district office personnel. Let's be clear however: it will take time,

Table 2.6 Unwrapping Standards

Standard	Knowledge	Reasoning	Performance	Product

effort, cooperation, and compromise. Start by building the shared decision that this is the right, first work to do when embracing RTI.

- Identify an area of the grade-level content (e.g., phonics, comprehension, number sense) or course (e.g., life science within biology, civilizations adapting to and modifying their environments within social studies).
- Commit that the products of teacher teams' work will not remain inert in binders on shelves.
- Commit that they will positively impact classrooms and student learning.

EFFECTIVE INSTRUCTION

Prioritizing the standards most essential for students to know, unpacking prioritized standards to drive instruction, and unwrapping prioritized standards to drive assessment is only the first step. Students will learn when they receive high-quality instruction and complete engaging tasks. Effective instructional practices have been defined and validated.

Meta-analyses (Hattie, 2009) have confirmed the efficacy of structured instructional models that include

- clear learning targets;
- clear descriptions of success at meeting targets;
- connections of new learning to existing schema and real life;
- modeling of new learning with a gradual release of responsibility to students;
- practice of new learning guided by the teacher with frequent checks for understanding and immediate, specific corrective feedback;
- closure during which teachers assess the lesson's success; and
- independent practice.

These elements neither need to be present in every lesson nor appear in the precise order in which they are listed above. In some instances, teachers will drive the pace and the process of instruction; in others, students will determine the pace and process of inquiry. The elements should, however, be present within the teaching and learning cycles that represent effective instruction in classrooms.

We want to make it clear that students must be thinking, talking, and working with one another, and solving authentic problems; the expectations of both 21st century workplaces and next-generation standards require these practices. The elements of effective instruction that we will describe are compatible with, and even require, inquiry, metacognition, and student collaboration.

The rationale for effective instruction starts with the need for a gradual release of responsibility for learning from teacher to student. At the beginning of units and lessons, the teacher assumes much of the responsibility, modeling problem solving and critical thinking through metacognitive modeling or thinking aloud. Students are then brought into the problem-solving and critical-thinking processes, with frequent give-and-take interactions; checks for understanding; and immediate, specific corrective feedback. Next, students solve problems with other students, receiving timely and targeted supports. Finally, new learning is reinforced through independent practice immediately following the lesson (Fisher & Frey, 2008; Hollingsworth & Ybarra, 2011; Hunter, 1982).

A gradual release of responsibility-type of lesson will not be effective unless it is focused and well defined; unless it is differentiated toward students' zones of proximal development; and unless it is relevant and connected to new learning (Piaget, 1970; Vygotsky, 1978). Therefore, we identify and communicate essential standards and unpack and unwrap targets so that instruction prepares students for mastery. In addition, we make explicit connections to existing schema and applications of learning so that knowledge becomes permanent. Finally, we check whether the release of responsibility was appropriately gradual and whether students have responded to the teacher's instruction; we assess the success of the lesson and students' progress toward mastery of the lesson's objective.

Following are descriptions of seven common-sense elements of effective instruction, never as important as they are today:

- What Are We Learning?
- Why Are We Learning It?
- I Do It.
- We Do It Together.
- You Do It Together.
- You Do It Alone.
- How Did We Do?

What Are We Learning?

Lessons with objectives that are too broad or ill-defined have little chance of success. When the sheer quantity of content that the class attempts to address in a lesson is too broad, teachers may move too quickly, have insufficient time to check for understanding, leave out explorations into greater levels of depth or complexity, and/or neglect to meet with small groups of students who require different types of supports and scaffolds. Students must have a crystal clear understanding of the focus of the lesson. Educators must make references to the lesson's objective throughout the learning process. Finally, the objectives must be related to students' current levels of readiness and needs.

Why Are We Learning It?

The teacher must also make clear connections to students' existing schema (Piaget, 1970) and to the world outside classrooms and schools. Teachers can and should connect the lesson's objective to lessons from prior years, units, weeks, and days. Teachers should describe how a lesson's objective will help prepare the class for future learning. Teachers will wisely place some of the responsibility for making connections between new learning and prior learning and students' experiences on students themselves. Learning will be inert and abstract unless teachers and students make connections.

I Do It.

Teachers must model the behaviors of an expert learner. Through enthusiastic and animated metacognitive modeling or think-alouds, teachers demonstrate the ways in which learning occurs for students; students have the opportunity to observe a model learner, the teacher, as the teacher metacognitively models critical thinking and problem solving. The quantity and quality of teacher talk is critical; teacher talk should be limited and should focus on demonstration and modeling. Students must clearly *see* and *hear* the thinking required for them to learn. Teachers often structure their think-alouds as self-dialogues that include *what* to do, *how* to do it, and *why* it's done. Steps are often necessary scaffolds for students as they learn new concepts. They are not intended to mechanize learning or to suggest that problem solving and critical thinking follow a rigid prescription. They can, however, provide students a foothold when they access new learning (Wood, Bruner, & Ross, 1976). Steps provide procedures students can rely on until they gain greater confidence and can include both words and pictorial supports. Graphic organizers are also tools whose use teachers may model and encourage students to use (Hattie, 2009; Marzano, Pickering, & Pollock, 2001). Today's students must increasingly articulate their mastery of content and concepts and justify their thinking; teacher modeling of articulating and justifying solutions, using tools such as graphic organizers, is more critical than ever.

We Do It Together.

Teachers and students must also solve problems together, starting with higher levels of teacher guidance, with students assuming more responsibility for their learning as checks for understanding reveal increasing levels of understanding. Students must have frequent opportunities to talk with one another (Bandura, 1977). The pace and progress of lessons should be based on evidence and feedback: Do checks for understanding indicate that students are *responding* to the teacher's *instruction?* When evidence gathered during frequent checks for understanding reveals errors, immediate, specific corrective feedback must follow (Duke & Pearson, 2002; Pearson & Gallagher, 1983). Student voice, student activity, and student engagement must be more present in classrooms than they are currently. A simple and effective way of engaging students, checking for understanding, and monitoring for the appropriate pace of the lesson is to employ think-pair-share strategies (Lyman, 1981).

You Do It Together.

Students should be provided with structured opportunities to work with and learn from their peers. Next-generation standards and the nature of 21st century skills both demand that students be provided with structured time to work with their peers, justifying their thinking, incorporating feedback, and critiquing the reasoning of their classmates, while receiving guidance from the teacher as they take responsibility for their own learning. Student interactions can begin simply: for instance, groups of students can individually complete a math problem before sharing results with partners. If all students agree, one student explains the method of solving the problem, explaining the how and the why, to other group members. If students have different answers, students representing the different solutions take turns presenting their solutions and students can identify and analyze errors. Or, groups of students can identify and contribute a cause or effect in relation to a key event in a story. These comprehension groups could then present their analysis to other small groups or to the entire class.

Tasks should be differentiated based on students' current levels or interests, as well as their interests; different groups of students choose from tasks that represent students' zones of proximal development. Alternatively, a teacher may determine that some students are not yet ready to be released to this level of responsibility. They may benefit from more guided practice, and the teacher may serve as the leader of a group of students who require more scaffolded support.

Teachers must equip students with the tools to assume the responsibility of negotiating their own learning with other students. Students collaborate, compromise, explain their thinking, and analyze errors. This appropriately places greater responsibility on students, but these interactions will not be productive without clear expectations that are modeled and practiced. Students of all ages can learn with and from their classmates when we set high and clear expectations.

You Do It Alone.

Homework has been a topic of controversy, but this need not be the case. Teachers must have evidence and confidence that students can complete You Do It Alone assignments, or homework, independently. These tasks should serve as a reinforcement of tasks completed during the lesson, cementing learning and assisting in the transfer from short-term to long-term memory (Anderson, 2000). If there is evidence that students are not ready to successfully and independently complete the planned homework, the teacher should assign an alternative set of tasks, or should assign no homework. Our knowledge of zones of proximal development and our knowledge of our students suggest that we should not be assigning the same tasks to all students. We acknowledge that we commonly have students in classes scoring in the fifth and in the ninety-fifth percentiles, and everywhere in between, on norm-referenced tests. We recognize that we should be differentiating instruction based on, among other factors, student readiness. It follows that we must assign different types of tasks as homework. These tasks should match the rigor and format of the types of tasks that students have completed throughout the lesson. A single homework assignment for all is bound to be a mismatch for two-thirds of students—those requiring more scaffolded support and those ready to extend their learning. We must differentiate tasks to match our differentiated instruction.

How Did We Do?

The success of a lesson can only be determined by the extent to which students have learned the topics, concepts, or skills that the teacher has taught. In other words, was the objective (the What are we learning?) met? A simple exit-slip or ticket-out-the-door can answer many important questions:

- How effective was the lesson's instruction?
- Does the class need to revisit topics, concepts, and skills during subsequent lessons?
- What patterns of errors are students making?
- Assuming the instruction was effective for most, which students are not yet responding?

As is the case with all assessments, students should be involved. One idea is to ask students to self-assess progress toward meeting the objective on a 1 to 5 scale, while also asking them to identify a simple strategy they will employ to continue their learning.

The research-based elements of effective instruction may not always proceed in the same order and they may be spread over multiple days, but they must be present. The best intervention is prevention, and the scaffolding and differentiation represented in the elements of effective instruction will ensure that more students are successful within core instructional blocks. Focus is key. The differentiated practice and depth of mastery that we must ensure that all students develop takes time. We will not have the time if we continue to race through textbooks or rigid curriculum maps. We must prioritize standards and map a set of outcomes that will viably be mastered by all students. Depth must be favored over breadth. Less is more. Table 2.7 illustrates intensive and cognitive planning for effective instruction.

MAPPING A UNIT OF INSTRUCTION

Larry Ainsworth (2010) defines unit mapping as "an inclusive set of intentionally aligned components—clear learning outcomes with matching assessments, engaging learning experiences, and instructional strategies—organized into sequenced units of study that serve as both the detailed road map and the high-quality delivery system for ensuring that all students achieve the desired end: the attainment of their designated grade- or course-specific standards within a particular content area." While Ainsworth describes the process as rigorous curriculum design, other educators have described processes for mapping a unit of instruction, from Heidi Hayes Jacobs (1997) with curriculum mapping, to Grant Wiggins and Jay McTighe (2005) with UbD. RTI must rest on a foundation in an intelligently mapped unit of instruction. There is neither doubt nor debate that the most critical tier of RTI is Tier 1—differentiated, focused, core instruction for all. RTI will never reach its potential unless we design and define a focused, guaranteed, and viable curriculum. In addition to

Table 2.7 Planning for Effective Instruction

What Are We Learning?

What are the essential standards of the unit?	What is the targeted, focused objective of this lesson?	What question can assess the success of the lesson?

Why Are We Learning It?

How does the lesson's objective connect to prior learning?	How does the lesson's objective connect to future learning?	How does the lesson's objective connect to real-world applications?

I Do It.

While solving and processing through problems before the lesson . . .

. . . slow your thinking and record the steps you followed.	. . . anticipate errors and misconceptions students may have and prepare to address them.	. . . identify any visual, tactile, kinesthetic, or mnemonic supports that will aid learning.

We Do It Together, You Do It Together, and You Do It Alone.

Locate and list tasks that match the rigor and format of the lesson's objective for students . . .

. . . requiring prerequisite supports and more scaffolds.	. . . on level, ready to engage with tasks and articulate their understanding.	. . . who have already begun to demonstrate mastery of the objective and are ready for enriched content.

(Continued)

Table 2.7 (Continued)

We Do It Together.

Students are prepared to participate in think-pair-share, with A–B partners and well-defined routines.	Student share-outs, including a more-formal mid-lesson check, will be used to determine the pace and direction of the lesson and to analyze errors . . .	. . . errors that will be explicitly identified and corrected in a positive spirit of continuous learning.

You Do It Together.

How has the class been prepared to work together in small groups with a high degree of autonomy?	How do students interact with other students and share their thinking with the class?	How do you identify students requiring more We Do It Together support? How do you provide this support?

How Did We Do?

What method of checking for the efficacy of the lesson do you employ (exit slip, ticket-out-the-door, clickers)?	What tasks, if any, are assigned to students if they are not ready to complete the planned homework (the You Do It Alone assignment)?	How do teachers and teacher teams use the evidence gathered during the How Did We Do? checks to inform future instruction?

the work of Ainsworth, Hayes Jacobs, Wiggins, and McTighe, Benjamin Bloom's Mastery Learning provides the inspiration and basis for our version of unit mapping:

1. Preassess for student mastery of foundational prerequisite skills of a content (or course, grade level, etc.) before or at the beginning of the year.

2. Prepare to provide Tier 3 interventions to identified students immediately upon the opening of the school year.

3. Prioritize standards and learning targets.

4. Unpack standards.

5. Unwrap standards.

6. Map prioritized standards into units.

7. Preassess for student mastery of a unit's immediate prerequisite skills.

8. Preteach the unit's immediate prerequisite skills prior to and at the beginning of the unit to students with the identified need.

9. Provide differentiated, Tier 1, direct instruction, with

   a. opportunities for students to deeply engage with complex tasks,
   b. supports for small groups of students with similar needs on a daily basis,
   c. frequent checks for understanding,
   d. immediate, specific feedback,
   e. administration of planned, periodic CFAs, and
   f. provision of Tier 2 supports for students requiring more time and alternative instructional strategies to master the prioritized standards while differentiated, Tier 1, direct instruction continues.

10. Administer and analyze end-of-unit assessments.

11. Provide Tier 2 supports for students requiring more time and alternative instructional strategies to master the prioritized standards of the completed unit while the new unit begins.

12. Repeat steps 3–11 for each unit.

Clearly, successfully following this process will require a great deal of focus on prioritized content, a focus that has not been achieved in the United States and Canada. Yet we must prioritize, we must focus, and we must embrace the process. The work of Benjamin Bloom, supported by recent analyses of the educational systems of international comparison countries that have followed Bloom's recommendations, dictate that for our students and for our societies, RTI is a moral and professional imperative.

SCHOOL CULTURE

Here are some challenges schools will face with regard to a universal approach at Tier 1:

- **My style is unique. A rigid pacing guide squashes my creativity.**

  We agree that a rigid pacing guide inhibits flexibility and opportunities to differentiate. We favor flexible pacing guides in which teacher teams agree on the prioritized standards that students must learn within a unit (e.g., a mathematics unit of twenty-two instructional days) and teams agree on the CFAs that will measure student progress within the unit (e.g., prior to the unit beginning, eleven days into the unit, and at the conclusion of the unit). The pace of the unit, and nature of the way in which teachers use the number of days, will depend on evidence of student learning. Teachers will make adjustments to strategies based on students' response to instruction. However, we must have pacing guides and CFAs to ensure a guaranteed, viable curriculum and to harness the collective power of our teams.

- **It's not my job to teach responsibility.**

  If it's not educators' responsibility to teach the social behaviors that students must display while at school, or to teach the academic behaviors that will enable them to learn how to learn, then whose responsibility is it? Do we expect parents to teach their children how to behave at school, whether socially or academically? The fact that educators have rarely explicitly defined, taught, reinforced, and remediated these behaviors does not mean we should not do so now. It has never been as critical for our students and our societies that educators embrace this responsibility and opportunity.

- **Students aren't motivated, and they have a sense of entitlement. There's nothing I can do.**

  Motivation is impacted by student attitudes, parental influence, and society at large. However, educators can have an enormous impact on student motivation. Students are motivated and engaged when they believe that standards are relevant, when they have choice, when they have relationships with teachers, when they have opportunities to collaborate with peers, when teachers model effective social and academic behaviors, and when schools nurture a growth mindset (Bandura, 1977; Covington, 1997; Dweck, 2006; Kuhl & Atkinson, 1986; Weiner, 2005). We can have a significant impact on student motivation if we accept responsibility for engaging students.

- **How do we manage change?**

  We know that some people are likely to resist change, and we know why. That we fail to respect the change process and appropriately and respectfully prepare our colleagues for change is a failure of professionalism and leadership. A fully realized form of RTI, so that student learning is powerfully impacted, will require that we do some things differently—that we refine the ways in which we educate children. What does social science report about the reasons people fear change?

- We fear failure.
- We are creatures of habit.
- We see no obvious need.
- We believe we will lose control.
- We are concerned about support.
- We believe that the new way may not be better.
- We fear the unknown.
- We are concerned about the personal impact.

Knowing that some may resist change, and knowing the reasons why they might resist change, we must lead change to anticipate and respect these legitimate concerns. We must

- thoroughly describe why the change is necessary;
- provide time for staff to study the *why* and the *what* of change;
- present balanced research on the effectiveness of proposed changes;
- provide the opportunity for staff to conduct their own research;
- provide the opportunity for staff to voice opinions;
- provide professional development regarding the new endeavor;
- establish a measure of the effectiveness of the new endeavor; and
- hold one another accountable for implementing the change.

When we do not respect our colleagues enough to respect the change process, we will not achieve the promises that change may deliver.

CHAPTER SUMMARY

Among the most critical initial and ongoing tasks of teacher teams are prioritizing standards, unpacking standards, unwrapping standards, employing effective instructional strategies, designing flexible units, and proactively and courageously addressing the culture of the school. These tasks are fundamental to RTI, to ensuring that all students—whether students with lower current levels of readiness, students on grade level, or students with more well-developed current levels of readiness—respond to initial instruction. Our traditional emphasis on breadth over depth, coverage over mastery, and teaching over learning have led to students requiring intervention; to students receiving failing grades and being retained; and to students being identified with a disability who were, in fact, simply denied a guaranteed, viable curriculum. We can and must think differently. We can and must do better.

The fundamental premises of all schools are a belief in all students, a belief that working together is the only way get it done, and that in highly effective schools, "Teachers and students go hand in hand as learners or they don't go at all" (Barth, 2001, p. 23).

Why? Because research shows collaboration results in higher levels of instant learning. Why? Because kids' lives are at stake. Why? Because it's our job.

3

Common Formative Assessments, Evidence, Data Analysis, and Collaboration

The best way to realize the full potential of RTI is through meaningful and engaging conversations amongst staff members. The more information we share about each student, the greater the likelihood we will identify the interventions that will produce positive results for each student. Collaboration is the key. In the absence of working together, there is a tendency for educators to believe that the solution lies in giving their best effort within the four walls of their classroom. This good intention dissuades any collective momentum being established and necessary breakthroughs from being achieved. Long-term, sustainable growth in schools is dependent on the creation of this collective response, regardless of the intervention tier or to the challenges that students face. National Commission on Teaching and America's Future (NCTAF) president Tom Carroll (2009, p. 13) takes it a step farther:

> Quality teaching is not an individual accomplishment, it is the result of a collaborative culture that empowers teachers to team up to improve student learning beyond what any of them can achieve alone. . . . The

idea that a single teacher, working alone, can know and do everything to meet the diverse learning needs of 30 students every day throughout the school year has rarely worked, and it certainly won't meet the needs of learners in years to come.

One of our most influential educators and researchers, John Hattie, conducted the most comprehensive study of factors affecting schooling ever compiled. He concluded that the most powerful strategy for helping students learn at higher levels was to ensure that teachers work collaboratively in teams to establish the essential learnings all students must acquire, to gather evidence of student learning through an ongoing assessment process, and to use the evidence of student learning to discuss, evaluate, plan, and improve their instruction (Hattie, 2009). All staff must be involved when determining appropriate levels of interventions and the particular strategies that will work for a child.

Rick DuFour (2011) speaks to the need to have our collaboration occur as part of a systematic approach, thereby ensuring that those students who need the most additional time and support receive it in a timely fashion. We intervene at the earliest opportunity, with an informed plan, and demonstrate that the plan is making a difference: "Rather than continuing with the education lottery, where what happens when a student experiences difficulty will depend almost solely on the individual teacher to whom that student is assigned, the school will create a multi-tiered, coordinated, and collective response to support that student" (DuFour, 2011, p. 13).

The notion of a guaranteed and viable curriculum (GVC) was advanced by Robert Marzano (2003). A school focused on ensuring a GVC would stress that the learning and skills considered essential are considered essential for *all* students. All members of the learning community would have a clear understanding of the concept of curriculum (the essential learning). This understanding allows educators to move away from the pursuit of the perfect textbook to drive instruction and instead to seek out materials they would use and instructional opportunities they would provide to ensure that *all* students reach the benchmarks set for the course or grade level. In order to effectively achieve this outcome, educators must have the time to collaborate and then use that time pursuing the outcomes that matter most. In his book *What Works in Schools*, Robert Marzano (2003, p. 34) states that his "Synthesis of research data reveals that a _guaranteed and viable curriculum_ is the school-level factor that has the most impact on student achievement yet it is probably the hardest to implement" (emphasis in original). By providing the necessary time to collaborate, schools and districts will enhance the possibility of achieving this outcome.

COLLABORATION AND COMMON FORMATIVE ASSESSMENTS

The sheer number of standards, combined with the need to create reliable assessment tools, renders the notion of teachers working in isolation impractical. To guarantee high levels of learning for all students as described above by

Hattie, DuFour, and Marzano, teachers need to work in teams. Creating quality CFAs in collaborative teams allows for this outcome to be achieved. Young (2009, p. 135) suggests that "formative assessments demand discussion about the best ways to help students learn the agreed-upon outcomes. They require consensus regarding the best way for students to demonstrate their learning." The assessments that are created must influence teachers' decision around instructional design and they must improve student learning. Stiggins and DuFour (2009, p. 641) explain

> collaborative teams of teachers create common assessments for three formative purposes. First, team-developed common assessments help identify curricular areas that need attention because many students are struggling. Second, they help each team member clarify strengths and weaknesses in his or her teaching and create a forum for teachers to learn from one another. Third, interim common assessments identify students who aren't mastering the intended standards and need timely and systematic interventions.

CFAs are absolutely critical in an RTI-inspired school. They provide the evidence of staff success and student learning; they inform the supplemental supports that will be necessary for some students to learn at high levels.

Nicole Vagle (2010; personal communication) has created an eight-step process for CFAs that also speaks to the need for collaboration. A modified version of her work appears here:

---

1. Establish and Maintain a Culture of Collaboration

   The school or teams establish a foundation for understanding the principles and work of a professional learning community and establish norms for working together:

   - What is the rationale and purpose for our work together?
   - What do we expect of one other?
   - How will we make decisions?
   - How will we resolve conflict or disagreement?
   - Do we understand how each member of our team processes and communicates information?
   - What do we believe about the contribution of each member?

2. Determine the Priority Standards

   Each grade level, course, or content area identifies prioritized standards. These essentials were chosen based on the criteria of endurance, leverage, readiness, connection to external assessments, and student needs. Teams plan CFAs around these priority standards. Tasks associated with prioritizing standards are described in the previous chapter.

3. Unwrap the Priority Standards

   Each grade level, course, or content area determines simple and complex learning targets that help guide the creation of assessments and define

   (Continued)

(Continued)

for students the learning targets that compose the standard. Tasks associated with unwrapping prioritized standards are also described in the previous chapter.

4. Create or Curate CFAs for the Unit

Each grade level, course, or content area crafts an assessment that measures the simple and complex learning targets of the unwrapped priority standards, including scoring guides and anchor solutions.

5. Create or Curate Common Formative Assessment(s)

Each grade level, course, or content area crafts assessments that will be administered in common within and at the completion of the unit. These assessments measure the simple and complex learning targets of the unwrapped priority standards and include scoring guides and anchor solutions to provide clarity around the rigor and format required for mastery. Assessments are designed to inform future instruction and intervention, checking on student mastery of the unwrapped priority standards that have been taught up to a given point of the unit.

6. Plan a Unit Map

Each grade level, course, or content area creates a calendar that identifies dates for preteaching, teaching, reteaching, and extensions, as well as for the team' administration, analyses, and responses of CFAs.

7. Analyze Common Assessment Data

Each grade level, course, or content area selects a data analysis protocol. Protocols guide teams in identifying targets that need more attention, help team members learn from areas of relative strength and weakness, and highlight students who have not yet mastered the prioritized standards.

8. Plan Response/Intervention

Each grade level, course, or content area team prepares to provide differentiated learning for extension and remediation:

- When will teams of teachers provide extensions and remediations?
- Which staff members will provide different types of supports?
- What strategies, approaches, and tasks will be used with extending and remediating?

9. Involve Students in Their Learning and the Assessment Process

Each grade level, course, or content area team determines how students will be active participants in their learning:

- Students track their progress on the learning targets and priority standards.
- Students reflect on what they do and do not understand.
- Students set goals and make plans regarding next steps toward mastery.
- Students receive and act on descriptive feedback.
- Students offer descriptive feedback to peers.
- Students assess their own work.

Source: Used by permission of Nicole Vagle.

COLLEGIALITY AND CONGENIALITY ARE NOT AS IMPACTFUL AS COLLABORATION

It may be helpful to delineate the differences between collegiality, congeniality, and collaboration. While the cooperative relationship of colleagues existing or associating together harmoniously are important for developing staff relationships and connections to a school, collegiality and congeniality fail to reach the impact that collaboration can have, and that high levels of learning for all students require. Without diminishing their relative importance to creating a positive school environment, collegiality and congeniality are easier to achieve and do not require as deep a level of commitment. School staffs' active participation in identifying what they value most requires a higher level of professionalism and sense of urgency than cooperation and good manners. As an example, many educators share the belief that all students can learn. However, in order for staff to actualize this learning, our behaviors need to mirror our intentions. If we really believe that all students can learn, then we will spend our time and effort on adult actions and behaviors that make learning a reality for all students. We'll steer clear of the time-wasting debates about zero as an earned grade or the unfairness of second chances. *All kids can learn* means we'll do whatever it takes to make that happen—not by lowering our standards, but by elevating all students to reach them, and by collaboratively planning interventions that will help kids close the gap. When two or more people work together to create or achieve the same goal and they are open to learning from each other, the potential to create the best plan is limitless. Reeves (2006, p. 26) sums it up: "We survive as a species and as leaders of organizations not due to solitary efforts but due to organizational and collaborative success."

Collaborative Teams

The term *collaborative team* describes the process by which educators make data-driven decisions at the classroom level. Professional learning communities (DuFour, DuFour, Eaker, & Many, 2011) provide an action-oriented structure that focuses the response of educators on four critical questions:

1. What is it we want all students to learn?

2. How will we know when each student has mastered the essential learning?

3. How will we respond when a student experiences initial difficulty in learning?

4. How will we deepen the learning for students who have already mastered essential knowledge and skills?

When members of a professional learning community incorporate the practices of data teams, the gains for students dramatically increase. Data teams follow a specific five-step process to examine student work, apply effective instructional strategies (including interventions), and monitor student learning in response to strategies and interventions (Figure 3.1):

1. Collect and chart/display the data

2. Analyze data and prioritize needs

3. Establish SMART goals: set, review, revise

4. Select instructional strategies

5. Determine results indicators

Data teams require strong leadership to provide guidance, direction, vision, support, and feedback throughout the collaborative inquiry cycle. The collaborative practices of professional learning communities and data teams align well with the major aspects of a strong RTI approach.

Tier 1 in RTI calls for high-quality, differentiated instruction for all students. To meet this goal, teachers collaboratively examine evidence of student response to academic and behavioral supports to identify which instructional strategies have met student needs. When a student does not respond to focused, differentiated core instruction, schools must supplement core instruction with

Figure 3.1   Inquiry Cycle

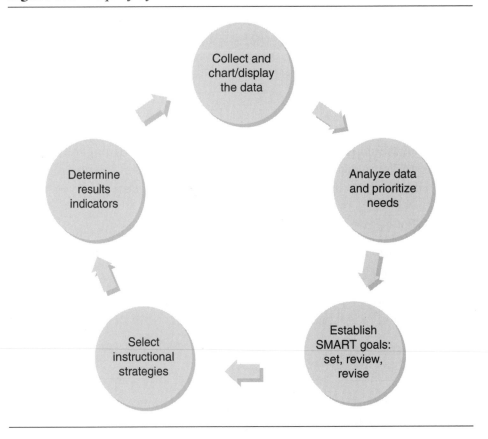

Tier 2 supports, whether the needs are academic or behavioral, or both. Whether this means more time, the use of alternative strategies, more frequency, smaller adult-to-student ratios, or more targeted interventions, the response must be derived from the data collected and the collaborative planning and analysis of all staff members. Decisions to increase the intensity of supplemental Tier 2 supports are based on evidence of a student's response to this focused intervention. Tier 2 and 3 supports must be provided *in addition to* high-quality, core instruction. Additional, supplemental interventions serve to augment core instruction, not supplant it. The steps of the inquiry cycle described above serve to guide teams in providing supplemental supports. When used within a framework RTI—in other words, when RTI is used as a *verb*—teams might repeat the inquiry cycle several times within a unit, so educators provide supports in a timely manner. Figure 3.1 can now be expanded to include the RTI cycle as shown in Figure 3.2.

Figure 3.2 adds a series of questions that we use as an extension of the inquiry cycle. These questions are shown in a useable table format in Table 3.1. Teams may use this format to identify students who may need additional supports or interventions as a result of the information yielded during team discussions.

RTI has a direct, parallel, and complementary relationship with the practices of collaborative teams. Just as RTI precludes a one-size-fits-all approach, collaborative teams assume that different instructional strategies will be required for students with different learning needs. The steps of the inquiry process help to continuously ground the core supports for students in the regular classroom provided by teacher teams; interventionists should not assume primary responsibility for a student's educational program. When students do not respond to supports that teachers teams provide, additional staff may join the teachers to problem solve, diagnose, and prescribe on behalf of students at risk. The Tier 2 and Tier 3 interventions that may be prescribed will be described in Chapters 5 and 6.

We refer to these additional staff members as the RTI team. The team may include any combination of the following:

- Principal
- Assistant principal
- Psychologist
- Social worker or counselor
- Special education staff
- Speech and language pathologist
- Occupational therapist
- Dean of student services (or comparable)

Some of these educators may also play an as-needed role on teacher teams as schools strive to achieve the best outcomes for their students. The success of teams parallels the success of supports, and both require strong leadership. The roles and responsibilities of the RTI team will be further described in Chapter 7.

Figure 3.2 Inquiry Cycle With Tiered Supports

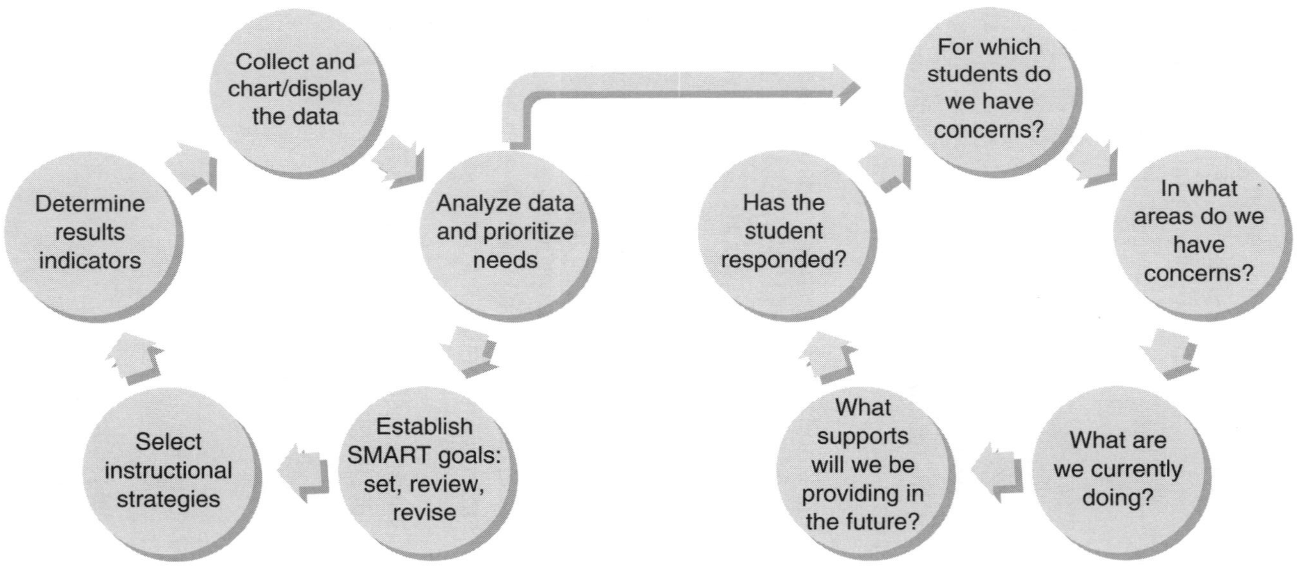

In what areas do we have concerns?

What are we currently doing?

For which students do we have concerns?

What supports will we be providing in the future?

Has the student responded?

Analyze data and prioritize needs

Collect and chart/display the data

Establish SMART goals: set, review, revise

Determine results indicators

Select instructional strategies

Table 3.1 Inquiry Cycle Questions

1. Which students do we have concerns about?				

2. In what areas do we have concerns?
  a. Academics
  b. Academic behaviors
  c. Social behaviors				

3. What are we currently doing to support the student and meet the student's needs?				
4. What supports will we be providing in the future?				
5. To what extent has the student responded to the instruction and interventions we have been providing?				

SCHOOL CULTURE

Cultural shifts that will be necessary when analyzing data and evidence from CFAs within collaborative inquiry teams include the following:

- **My collaboration time is mine. No one should tell me how to use that time.**

    In an era where educators feel overwhelmed by the demands on their time (and next-generation standards and assessments may be adding to these demands), the desire to be left alone is strong. A typical teacher might respond by wanting to remain within the four walls of the classroom, to just focus on "my kids and my time." The reality is that the more educators inform their practice through the exchange of best practices, the work can become less stressful and feelings of professional isolation less debilitating. Staff members need to collaboratively generate the solutions for their students. Collaboration time is best used to discuss teaching and learning and should not be wasted on less-professionally oriented tasks or simply on identifying problems for others to solve.

- **I know what works best for my kids.**

    All students who cross the threshold of your school are your responsibility. While each educator has a particular assignment, there must be a collective commitment to the success of *all* kids . . . not just *my* kids. Let's break away from pockets of excellence to schools of excellence. Let's share successes and effective practices rather than hoard what's working as a personal item. "My Best Lesson" ought to be a feature at all schools, allowing colleagues to learn from each other.

- **RTI seems like the latest fad in education. I think it will be replaced by another soon enough.**

    If RTI is simply part of a compliance piece at your school in response to legislation or other external forces, it will be a passing fad like many seen in education. If it seems like more work or an add-on, it probably is. If instead it is part of what you do to ensure the highest levels of success for all students—a framework through which students reach their fullest potential—it will become part of the "way we do things around here." We've never heard educators complain about doing the work if the work is the right pursuit. Cynics in schools today exist because we've been guilty of initiating too many misaligned pursuits or quick fixes. RTI is neither a misaligned pursuit nor a quick fix; it will require the collective efforts of all educators at your site to impact all students.

- **Data will just be used against me so I'm better served by having as little as possible.**

    The concept of data has taken on a negative meaning in education over the last decade as it has been either misused (only to rank and sort students and educators) or not used at all ("Why are collecting this information?"). The route past this dilemma is to turn data into evidence that impacts the teaching–learning cycle. Using data to engage the collective conversation about "our students" requires leaders to adjust their views of data and what it may indicate. Focusing on the growth aspect of each student (and educator) allows for a positive view of the data collected.

CHAPTER SUMMARY

One of the key components of achieving the intended outcomes of an effective RTI approach is to have parents and students as partners. This becomes easier to achieve when educators possess the data and support information to be able to clearly articulate students' needs and validate the "why" of RTI. Teams help pinpoint the data that are relevant for each student as we collaboratively create the plan for future success. The key role that collaboration plays cannot be understated in any of the areas required for students to reach their maximum level of success—instructional design, assessment, and interventions. Collaborative teams that are empowered, knowledgeable, and accountable can meet student needs more comprehensively and with a greater level of professional fulfillment than can any individual working in isolation.

Information Within RTI

Screening, Progress Monitoring, and Diagnoses

We are committed to doing whatever it takes to ensure that all K–12 students learn at high levels—levels that will lead to students graduating ready for postsecondary opportunities or a skilled career. To achieve this goal, we must be informed about student strengths and needs. And so we face a significant paradox: Some say we assess too frequently and that assessment takes too much time, and yet we lack sufficient information needed to meet students' needs and inform instruction. How might we resolve this paradox? Teams would start by

1. inventorying current assessments to ensure that they are necessary to inform your practice, and

2. embracing the notion that instruction and assessment are two sides of the same critical coin.

These two topics are the themes of this chapter.

In Chapter 3, the products of assessments—data—were the primary focus. Data analyses, collaboratively driven by teacher teams with a sense of urgency for student success, are the engines that drive schools. In this chapter we will provide details on the types of assessments that produce data. If we do not intelligently, frequently, and flexibly assess, we can neither determine whether students are responding to instruction and intervention nor make the adjustments that will undoubtedly be necessary.

SCREENING

"Universal screening" has become a buzzword and common practice of schools. Do teachers know *why* they administer screening measures, though? And do schools act on the knowledge that these measures provide? In our experiences, the answer to both questions is no.

We administer screening measures to identify students who are significantly at risk for failure and difficulties before the school year is under way. In fact, to suggest that students who lack knowledge of foundational prerequisite skills are at risk is a terrible understatement. Students with significant deficits in literacy, mathematics, or behavior will experience significant challenges, even when teachers scaffold and differentiate access to grade-level or course content. We must scaffold and differentiate instruction so that students have access to content, *and* we must provide immediate, intensive supports in foundational prerequisite skills when screening reveals that such deficits exist.

Screening need not be time-intensive, and it does not require a separate test. Screening requires that we gather information on all students regarding their known abilities in literacy, mathematics, and behavior. Staff should never end their school year in May or June without a near-perfect list of names of the students who will require immediate, intensive supports in foundational prerequisite skills come the beginning of the next school year. Incoming Kindergarten students can, and should, be registered and screened prior to the end of the school year. Information on incoming middle school (or junior high) and high school students can, and should, be gathered prior to the end of the school year. We should only lack universal screening knowledge for students who newly enroll in our school.

A few quick words about students that are newly enrolling in a school: If it's predictable, it's preventable. We can predict that a large number of students transitioning to a new school will experience some challenges. We should not be surprised. Schools can and should train office staff to administer simple screens to new students when their parents enroll them. Schools can and should act on this knowledge with supports as necessary. At a minimum, schools should arrange for social supports to students—perhaps, most appropriately and successfully, supports provided by other students.

Staff can also administer universal screening measures at the beginning of the school year; when wisely selected, these beginning-of-the-year measures provide timely information on where students stand in relation to well-researched benchmarks. Because many of these measures are administered in one-on-one settings, they allow staff to interact with students and can even be used as preliminary diagnoses. RTI literature often recommends that universal screening measures be administered three times per school year (at the beginning, middle, and end of the school year), and in early grades, when development of skills is rapid, a mid-year measure may be appropriate. Yet let's not forget why we're administering universal screening measures: we want to identify students who, in the absence of immediate, intensive supports, will experience difficulties.

We *cannot* predict that a student will have difficulty learning about meiosis in a seventh-grade science unit in February when they have otherwise understood science concepts well. We *can* predict that a seventh-grade student reading at the third-grade level will have difficulty reading about meiosis in science texts, and learning in all subjects. We *cannot* predict that a student will be confused about the appropriate signs of answers when adding, subtracting, multiplying, and dividing integers in late elementary and middle school grades, even though that student understands other number sense concepts well. We *can* predict that a late elementary and middle school student who does not possess absolute automaticity with basic, single-digit computation will constantly and consistently struggle when trying to learn mathematics. We *cannot* predict that a student will struggle connecting with the themes of a text. We *can* predict that students who cannot write coherent sentences and do not have the basics of subject–verb agreement and punctuation in place will not be able to express their understanding in writing, no matter the class or course. We *cannot* predict that a student's parents will divorce, or that an illness will lead to an extended absence; both scenarios will lead to behavioral, social, or emotional needs, impacting a student's learning. We *can* predict a student with a history of more than twenty absences or multiple suspensions will be at risk in the coming year and we can take steps to positively connect with these students and their families immediately on the opening of the school year. Screening guides us to identify students significantly at risk so that we can provide immediate, intensive supports.

Table 4.1 lists a few simple measures and supports that can be used to screen for deficits in foundational prerequisites.

Universal screening measures are preliminary assessments that allow us to provide preventative supports. They are similar in this manner to pre-assessments that may be administered prior to units of instruction.

Pre-Assessments

While we may devote more time than ever to assessments, assessment done wisely can actually save instructional time. Consider pre-assessments as an example. When we assess students' existing knowledge of content that they will learn in an upcoming unit, we have the opportunity to identify what content will require additional time and what content can be compacted, or addressed in an abbreviated amount of time. As we increasingly differentiate for individuals, groups, and entire classes, clarity regarding the consolidation of content to gain additional instructional time is incredibly valuable. The ability to compact instruction will allow teachers and students to delve more deeply into other content, using precious time more efficiently. Alternatively, schools may administer pre-assessments that determine the extent to which students possess the prerequisite skills necessary to master content in the

Table 4.1 Measures

Skill Area	Measures	School Response
Literacy	<ul><li>State Tests</li><li>Northwest Evaluation Association (NWEA) Measures of Academic Progress (MAP)</li><li>Dynamic Indicators of Basic Early Literacy Skills (DIBELS)</li><li>Scholastic Reading Inventory (SRI)</li><li>STAR Reading</li><li>AIMSweb</li></ul>	Tier 3 supports automatically in the school schedule
Mathematics	<ul><li>State Tests</li><li>Northwest Evaluation Association (NWEA) Measures of Academic Progress (MAP)</li><li>IXL</li><li>Scholastic Math Inventory (SMI)</li><li>STAR Math</li><li>AIMSweb</li></ul>	Tier 3 supports automatically in the school schedule
Behavior	<ul><li>Referrals</li><li>Behavior documentation forms and teacher feedback</li><li>Poor attendance</li><li>Student Risk Screening Scale (SRSS)</li><li>Student Internalizing Behavior Screening Scale (SIBSS)</li></ul>	Immediate positive check in/ check out (CICO)
Grades	<ul><li>D or F grades</li><li>Low homework completion</li></ul>	Immediate study skills support

upcoming unit, informing which students and which prerequisite skills require preteaching. If schools build time to provide preteaching supports into schedules, giving teachers advanced knowledge of which students require preteaching support and the prerequisite skills in which they lack understanding, educators can provide proactive, preventative supports.

If it's predictable, it's preventable. We can predict that there will be students who already possess substantial knowledge of upcoming content and students who lack immediate and foundational prerequisite skills. Without knowledge of the students and their skills we cannot hope to provide preventative supports. Perhaps districts and schools already require that teachers administer pre-assessments, but staff is not certain why they give these tests. Or, perhaps staff knows why they give these tests, but schools do not provide time for the collaborative analysis of the results. Screening and pre-assessments are both preventative, predictive assessments. To ensure that there is time available for their productive use, we must inventory the assessment we administer.

Inventory Assessments

Consider these lofty goals:

- We will not administer formal assessments that we do not collaboratively administer.
- We will not administer formal assessments for which time is not devoted for the collaborative analysis of results.
- We will not administer formal assessments that do not immediately inform instruction.

To meet these goals, to effectively manage the instruction/assessment balance, and to glean the information we require to meet the needs of all students, we must be much more thoughtful about the assessments we administer. Consider these questions:

- What data do we need?
- What assessments yield that data?
- How will data lead to information that leads to continuous adjustments and improvements to instruction?

We must address the paradox that represents so many educators' thinking about testing—we give too many assessments but require more information to meet our goal of high levels of learning for all students. How do we avoid suffering from DRIP (data rich, information poor)? The template in Table 4.2 will assist teams and schools when they evaluate the assessments they give.

If there are redundancies, we must choose the assessment that yields the best information in the most efficient manner. If an assessment yields loads of data that we simply cannot use to inform instruction, we must consider abandoning these tests. If tests are given solely for the purpose of averaging grades or filling out a report card—if they do not also inform instruction—we must

Table 4.2   Analyzing Your Sources of Data

What information do we need?	What assessments do we administer?	Are there redundancies?	Are there gaps?

Connection to RTI

There is no RTI—no response to instruction and intervention without determining whether students are responding. To make this determination, we must assess and analyze.

consider informing grades using assessments that also inform teaching and learning, combined with evidence of student learning that teachers gather every day.

Common Formative Assessments

CFAs, well designed and unwrapped so they are designed to measure the types of understanding that we want students to master, are an invaluable contributor to RTI data. When collaboratively created or curated, collaboratively administered, and collaboratively analyzed to inform instruction, they can be among the most powerful initiatives a school can embrace.

> Assessment for learning . . . when done well . . . is one of the most powerful, high-leverage strategies for improving student learning that we know of. Educators collectively at the district and school levels become more skilled and focused at assessing, disaggregating, and using student achievement as a tool for ongoing improvement. (Fullan, 2006, p. 71).

> Effective use of formative assessment, developed through teacher learning communities, promises not only the largest potential gains in student achievement but also a process for affordable teacher professional development. (Wiliam & Thompson, 2007, p. 67)

> Studies have demonstrated assessments for learning rivals one-on-one tutoring in its effectiveness, and that the use of assessment particularly benefits low-achieving students. (Stiggins, 2007, p. 27)

We are not exaggerating when we submit that CFAs are proven tools that can dramatically improve student learning. While educators may agree with this sentiment, and while research supports this assertion, how do CFAs support RTI?

As we described earlier in this chapter, universal screening measures can help schools predict students who lack foundational prerequisite skills, and they can proactively prevent students beginning a school year without support plans in place. We also described how pre-assessments administered before the beginning of units can help schools to predict which students lack immediate prerequisite skills, allowing us to proactively preteach students before, and at the beginning of, new units.

> ### Connection to RTI
>
> Well-written, well-designed assessments more accurately identify students who need assistance and why they need the assistance. When analyzed well, they validate Tier 1 supports for most students and provide the details needed to provide timely reteaching to others.

Universal screening measures and pre-assessments may not, however, predict which students may experience difficulties mastering new content within new units. Benjamin Bloom established the concept of Mastery Learning to anticipate these occurrences. We can be prepared to meet the needs of students who experience difficulties within units, and we can predict that there will be such students.

CFAs, both those administered during and at the conclusion of units, can answer three critical questions when collaboratively analyzed by teacher teams:

- Who has not yet learned the prioritized standards within the unit?
- For what specific standards, and skills within these standards, must the teacher devote more time and employ different approaches?
- Which teacher on the team has had more relative success with these standards and skills?

  - If there is not a teacher on the team who has had more success, are there teachers within the broader school system whom we can contact? or
  - What external resources, strategies, or professional development can we access?

We will detail the who, when, and what of reteaching prioritized standards and skills in the next chapters. Without CFAs, administered and analyzed through teacher teams, we lack the timely and specific evidence we need to inform these targeted supports.

We cannot overstate this critically important point: Whereas assessment for learning and assessment as learning are powerful levers for dramatically improving student achievement, they will not occur without greater focus. Whereas screening, preassessments, and CFAs are research based to improve and deepen all students' learning, they take time. We will not have the time if we continue to race through the curriculum—if we do not focus on student mastery of the most highly prioritized content, and if we do not collaboratively plan for a guaranteed, viable curriculum as described in Chapter 2.

PROGRESS MONITORING

It's very simple: there is simply no RTI unless we check on whether students are *responding* to intervention. We check on whether students are responding to supports through a process known as progress monitoring. There are essentially three types of progress monitoring.

The first type of progress monitoring is designed for students who have been screened or determined to lack foundational prerequisite skills, typically in the foundational skills of reading or mathematics. Monitoring progress to ensure that students are responding to the intensive interventions that are likely provided in these cases is most accurately and efficiently accomplished using curriculum-based measurements (CBMs). CBMs that are used for progress monitoring are often the same assessments used for screening in the early grades. There are free or low-cost CBM options available in specific skill areas listed in Table 4.3. When using CBMs, progress should be monitored frequently—every one to two weeks—depending on the level of concern for student needs. The CBM that teams select should, as much as possible, match

- the instructional level at which the student is receiving support, which will likely not be the student's grade level, at least when the teacher first provides supports; and
- the skill with which the student is receiving support.

Table 4.3   Curriculum-Based Measurement Options

Area in Which Student Is Receiving Support	Measures

Reading	- Phonological awareness
	  o Initial sound fluency
	  o Phoneme segmentation fluency
	- CVC (Consonant-Vowel-Consonant) phonics
	  o Nonsense or pseudoword word fluency
	- CCVC or CVCC Phonics
	  o Nonsense or pseudoword word fluency
	- Fluency
	  o Oral reading fluency
	- Vocabulary
	  o A timed cloze assessment, such as MAZE or DAZE
	- Comprehension
	  o Qualitative Reading Inventory

Mathematics	- Counting and cardinality
	  o Early numeracy probes
	  o Computation probes
	- Fractional awareness
	  o Decompose shapes
	  o Name the fraction for a picture
	  o Produce equivalent fractions
	  o Compare fractions and decimals
	  o Decompose fractions
	- Word problems
	  o Write expression and equation probes

A typical length of time to monitor progress before making adjustments is six to eight weeks. This is primarily due to the fact that a statistical trend cannot be made with confidence without six to eight data points. However, six to eight weeks is a guide; if team members believe that there is a clear indication that supports are not appropriate sooner, then they should make a change on behalf of the student. If there is evidence that the support has had a significantly positive impact, and less intervention is appropriate, then they should make a change on behalf of the student. If six to eight weeks have elapsed and team members believe that more time can make the difference or that changes aside from the selection of another intervention will make the difference, then they can continue providing supports. Rigid decision processes are not in students' best interests. We will address RTI team decision making more fully in Chapter 7.

For the second type of progress monitoring, there are not pre-packaged assessments widely available. When CFAs reveal that students require more time and an alternative approach to master prioritized standards, the most appropriate progress monitoring assessment is simply another version of the pre-assessment or CFA, to ensure that the student has achieved mastery.

An obstacle that schools often face is an overall unwillingness to provide students with these opportunities. We address these cultural concerns at the conclusion of this chapter, but let us be clear: We are deluding ourselves if we believe we can expect that all students can learn without anticipating that some students will require additional time. We are not being honest with ourselves and with students and their families if we express that we are willing to do whatever it takes, but then are not willing to provide students with (or do not *require* students to take advantage of) additional opportunities to prove their mastery. We are not implementing RTI if there is a not a systematic expectation and opportunity for this type of progress monitoring.

There will not be a CBM that is appropriate for every area in which we are providing interventions. We need not complicate progress monitoring for mastery of prioritized standards. There will not be CBMs for these purposes; alternative versions of pre-assessments and CFAs can satisfy this need.

The third type of progress monitoring is used to check on the appropriateness of behavioral supports. A process of Check In, Check Out, or CICO, is the most appropriate and widely accepted manner of monitoring the progress of behavioral interventions. While there are commercially available CICO options, the sample in Figure 4.1 provides schools with the tool they need.

There are several key features of CICO. First, a staff member has been identified to CICO with the student. The criterion for selecting this staff member is willingness—a willingness to have a positive relationship with the student. The staff member checks in with the student before school:

How was your afternoon? How many points did you earn yesterday? What was one thing that went well yesterday? What was one thing that could have gone better? What is your goal for today? Have a great day, and good luck on your math test. See you after school!

Figure 4.1   Check In/Check Out

Check In/Check Out for _____ (Student)

Check In/Check Out with _____ (Staff Member)

Date:

Today, I am working on

This is how I did today:

    3 = Great!   (I was reminded to be on task 0 or 1 times)

    2 = Pretty good (I was reminded to be on task 2 or 3 times)

    1 = So-so   (I was reminded to be on task more than 3 times)

Times of the Day	Specific Skill: _____	
	Student	**Staff**

Today I earned _____ points.

When I earn _____ points or more, I earn _____.

The staff member then checks out with the student after school, reviewing the student's CICO sheet:

> Let's take a look at your sheet. I notice that you and Ms. Harris disagree about how well you did in reading. Can you tell me about that? What are you most proud of today? What could have gone better? How was your math test? What are you doing after school? How many points did you earn today? What's your goal for tomorrow?

Students are the primary driver of this process. Among our goals is to help them build better habits, to allow them to reflect on their behaviors, and to help them self-monitor.

Another key feature of the CICO sheet is to identify a specific behavioral skill upon which the student and staff will focus. It is critical that we have collaboratively investigated the specific behavioral skill that requires attention, and why and when the behaviors are occurring. It is also critical that staff has reiterated expectations, and that staff has provided strategies and reteaching. The specific, target skill must be clear. A target such as "improved behavior" is not sufficiently specific. More information will be provided on diagnosing behavior in the next section, "Diagnoses."

Part of the power of behavioral interventions lies in the process of checking in and checking out—that is, through the process of progress monitoring. The progress monitoring of a student's performance is a critical part of the intervention in all areas of need.

DIAGNOSES

The best interventions specifically target the antecedents to student difficulties. If we can discover why a student is falling short of expectations, then we are more likely to help the student be successful. We too often provide general, one-size-fits-all programs that promise to improve entire content areas, such as "reading" or "fourth-grade mathematics." While there may be a place for these types of interventions, students with significant deficits will respond most rapidly to supports that target the specific skills that are inhibiting their progress. The more diagnostic and specific the assessments, the more targeted, specific, and successful the intervention will be. Although diagnosing student needs can be time-consuming, and diagnostic interviews are often conducted in one-on-one settings, we are not diagnosing all students, but only those students in need of assistance. We diagnose to determine what specific supports are necessary. It will take time, but it's only for students about whom we have concerns and questions and who require interventions to be on track to graduate ready for postsecondary opportunities or a skilled career.

This is certainly not to suggest that we delay providing supports until we have complete, exhaustive, and extensive diagnoses. Students at risk cannot afford to wait while we schedule, administer, and analyze these assessments. We learn so much about their needs through the process of intervening. A diagnose-prescribe-diagnose approach will provide students at risk with immediate supports, allow us to rule out possible explanations for poor performance, and provide further insights into student thinking.

There may be diagnostics that educators can purchase, but the most effective diagnostics come from information gathered through structured interviews with students. To illustrate the diagnose-prescribe-diagnose and provide a sample of diagnostic interviews, consider this example:

The most likely area of deficit for a student is reading. If students can read connected text—that is, if they can identify and read words in a passage—and yet teachers are concerned about their reading abilities, we recommend initiating supports through oral reading fluency. While a student reads a passage, use the diagnostic interviews in Tables 4.4 (fluency) and 4.5 (phonics).

If the student's reading rate is poor and there exists a pattern and/or number of errors that contribute to a poor rate, then the student's most immediate area of need may be phonics; a diagnostic interview in phonics may identify the most appropriate targeted supports.

Table 4.4 Diagnostic Interview: Fluency

Task	Notes
Listen to the student read for 60 seconds.	
Record errors using the school's agreed-on running records format.	
Note the student's words correct per minute.	
Note the number of student errors.	
Note any pattern of errors (long vowels, multisyllabic words, etc.)	
Note the prosody/expression with which the student reads: 1 = reading is labored, slow, and dis-fluent; 2 = reading is somewhat slow and choppy; 3 = reading includes poor phrasing and intonation, but is at a reasonable pace; 4 = reading is fairly fluent, with good pace, fairly good intonation, and some phrasing; or 5 = reading is fluent and smooth with longer phrasing, good intonation, and varied expression.	

Table 4.5   Diagnostic Interview: Phonics

Task	Notes
Present student with the requisite letters, pseudowords, or words and note the success with which the student . . .	
Produces letter names when presented with letters.	
Produces consonant sounds when presented with letters.	
Produces long vowel sounds when presented with letters.	
Produces short vowel sounds when presented with letters.	
Reads (blends/decodes) CVC words.	
Reads (blends/decodes) words and pseudo-words with short vowels and consonant blends at the beginning of and end of the word.	
Reads (blends/decodes) words and pseudo-words with short vowels and consonant digraphs and trigraphs at the beginning of and end of the word.	
Reads (blends/decodes) CVCe words.	
Reads (blends/decodes) words and pseudo-words with other long vowel sound spellings.	

Task	Notes
Reads (blends/decodes) words and pseudo-words with r-controlled vowels.	
Reads (blends/decodes) words and pseudo-words with vowel diphthongs.	
Reads (blends/decodes) multisyllabic words and pseudo-words, both with closed syllable types.	
Reads (blends/decodes) multisyllabic words and pseudo-words, with closed and VCe syllable types.	
Reads (blends/decodes) multisyllabic words and pseudo-words, with open and -e syllable types.	
Reads (blends/decodes) multisyllabic words and pseudo-words, with open and closed syllable types.	
Reads (blends/decodes) multisyllabic words and pseudo-words, with vowel team syllable types.	
Reads (blends/decodes) multisyllabic words and pseudo-words, with r-controlled-vowel syllable types.	
Reads (blends/decodes) multisyllabic words and pseudo-words, with consonant -le syllable types.	

If the student's reading rate is poor, and yet the ability to decode and attack words seems solid, then an intervention that focuses on improving fluency, reading rate, and prosody may be most appropriate. If neither rate nor accuracy seems to be a concern, and yet the student's reading performance is still a concern, then interventions in the area of vocabulary and comprehension may be necessary.

The potential power and simplicity of diagnostic interviews is perhaps most noticeable in mathematics and behavior, areas in which teachers and schools may have less experience with diagnostic assessment. In early mathematics, a student's inability to solve problems can be attributed to several specific sets of skills that we can identify; once we have identified those sets of skills, we can remediate them. The diagnostic interview in Table 4.6 can be used to determine areas of need for younger students.

When students are experiencing later difficulties in mathematics, the diagnostic interview in Table 4.7 can assist in identifying where the problem solving is breaking down.

Diagnostic interviews can help teachers and schools determine the types of supports that will allow the student to positively and adequately respond to both initial instruction and supplemental interventions. We have the professional knowledge to meet students' needs; our success is often limited by an inability to know the targeted areas in which students most require support.

It is in the area of behavior that our interventions and supports have been, perhaps, the least targeted and least successful. Determining what is leading to student misbehavior is absolutely critical. The diagnostic interview in Table 4.8, based on an analysis of the function of misbehaviors, will provide teams with the information they need to identify specific supports.

The diagnostic interview for behavior is particularly normative and beneficial when misbehaviors are related to acting out, when students' misbehaviors are externalizing in nature, and when student difficulties relate to social behaviors such as cooperation and respect.

In our experiences, the two most common behavioral difficulties with which students experience challenges are motivation and attention. A diagnostic interview for motivation is provided in Table 4.9.

When a diagnostic interview reveals areas of need for a particular student, we must address these deficits. Yet as we examine students with deficits in the area of motivation, with attributes such as those described in Table 4.9, we must ask ourselves whether we provide initial instruction to *all* students in these areas; whether we model these behaviors; and whether our tasks, assessment practices, and learning environments support a growth mindset instead of a fixed mindset; we must reflect on our core practices for all. To what extent are we consistently reinforcing and motivating positive learning?

Inattention and lack of motivation in students negatively impacts learning. To help students improve in these areas, we must first accept responsibility for assisting students in these areas. Then we must know what is represented by motivation, how we can assess deficiencies, and how we can adopt practices and create environments that support core and supplemental supports for higher levels of attention and motivation.

Table 4.6 Diagnostic Interview: Early Mathematics

Possible Tasks	Notes
Present student with the requisite numbers or worksheets and ask the student to . . .	
Identify numbers.	
Write a given number.	
Represent a given number with objects.	
Identify and/or write the number that presents a quantity that is represented by objects.	
Identify which set of objects represents greater value.	
Count, beginning at different values.	
Identify and/or write the missing value in a sequence.	

Table 4.7   Diagnostic Interview: Mathematics

Possible Tasks	Notes
Select and present target problems. Be prepared to use the progression and coherence of next-generation standards such as the CCSS to assign problems from prior grade levels. And . . .	
Ask the student to orally describe how to plan to solve the problem.	
Ask the student to begin solving the problem.	
Ask *why* and *how* questions at every step of the problem-solving process: Why do you set up the problem in that way? Why did you take that step? How did you figure out the answer? How did you decide that was the answer?	
Ask the student to visually represent the problem (drawing, graph, bar model, array, rectangular model, circular model).	
Cocreate a visual representation *with* the student or create a visual representation *for* the student, and ask the student to interpret.	
Ask the student why the answer makes sense.	
Ask the student to describe a similar problem.	
Examine where the student's problem solving seems to breaking down: • Sense of number • Computation • Use of the algorithm • Application of the procedures or steps • Understanding of the concept • Organization of the work, such as if the student is sloppy or imprecise.	

Table 4.8   Diagnostic Interview: Behavior

Questions for the *Team* and/or the *Student* and/or the *Parent*	Notes
Clearly, specifically, and objectively define and describe the problem behavior.	
Identify the consequence or reinforcement the student receives due to the misbehavior. (Be honest . . . even if our responses to misbehavior may not be entirely appropriate, e.g., raising our voices or removing students from the classroom.)	
Identify what the student seems to be seeking by misbehaving. What is the function or purpose of the misbehavior? Does this student seem to be seeking sensory feedback? Does the student seem to be attempting to avoid or escape from a task or situation? Does the student seem to be seeking attention? Does the student seem to be attempting to gain a tangible object or experience? Be as specific and detailed as possible.	
Define the behaviors, actions, and/or words that immediately precede the misbehavior. Are there behaviors, actions, and/or words that the student tends to exhibit before the undesirable behaviors manifest?	

(Continued)

Table 4.8 (Continued)

Questions for the *Team* and/or the *Student* and/or the *Parent*	Notes
Define the environments, times of day, subject areas, groupings, and/or assignment types during which the misbehavior is most likely to occur. What is the student doing or being asked to do? Where is the student? Who is the student with?	
Define an alternative behavior that staff would accept on a temporarily basis that would satisfy the student's need and that would likely meet the purpose or function the misbehavior has been meeting. What options with which the teacher is comfortable can staff give to the student?	
Clearly reteach the desired and acceptable behavior that the student will optimally display. Clearly define, describe, and model for the student and teacher what the desired behavior looks like and sounds like.	
Define the reinforcement the student will temporarily receive (until a new habit has been established) for displaying the desired and acceptable behavior. What tangible positive reinforcement will be meaningful to the student when the most desired behavior is produced?	
Consider administering a more-specific diagnostic interview, e.g., for attention or motivation, particularly if the student does not respond to initial interventions.	

Table 4.9   Diagnostic Interview: Motivation

Questions for the *Team* and/or the *Student* and/or the *Parent*	Notes
Describe the extent to which the student employs metacognitive practices (reflections and beliefs about their thinking) to school and to everyday life: • Makes connections between new and old learning • Relates school to life experiences • Relates topics from one subject area to another • Rehearses learning with self and others • Identifies the skills needed to make meaning of new learning	
Describe the student's self-concept (e.g., seeing self as smart): • Believes in her or his ability to be successful in school • Attributes success on a test to effort • Confidently answers all test questions to the best of her or his ability • Believes that success is due to internal forces that are controllable, not external forces that cannot be affected; learned helplessness is absent • Believes that others will judge her or him as competent and confident due to effort	
Describe the student's skill at self-monitoring (ability to plan and prepare): • Arranges and initiates steps for completing tasks • Assesses performance and progress toward a goal • Establishes and adjusts work rate so that he or she meets the goal by the established time • Quizzes self periodically to summarize and process learning	
Describe the student's engagement (ability to maintain interest): • Loves being in school • Studies all subjects with the same enthusiasm • Perseveres when work is difficult • Sets short-term goals • Spends time with friends and socializes only after work is finished • Is driven to succeed, not to avoid failure • Pursues learning for the sake of learning; intent on mastering tasks and acquiring skills—not simply on performing, proving adequacy, or avoiding failure	

(Continued)

Table 4.9 (Continued)

Questions for the *Team* and/or the *Student* and/or the *Parent*	Notes
Describe the student's use of learning strategies (techniques for organization and memorization): • Rehearses prior learning • Elaborates on current learning • Makes drawings to aid understanding • Learns new words or ideas by thinking about a situation in which they occur • Translates new ideas into own words • Employs multiple strategies to learn new material • Prepares for tests with focus	
Describe the student's volition (effort needed to stay motivated): • Keeps studying until finished even when the work seems less than exciting • Completes tasks with a plan and on time, not waiting until the last minute • Concentrates fully when studying, setting aside a length of time and sticking to it • Modifies learning environments to facilitate success and decrease distractions • Obtains and maintains the necessary materials and aids to achieve a goal • Stops from responding to distractors and delays gratification until achieving a goal	
Describe the student's ability to control emotions (techniques for regulating response to situations): • Views challenges and mistakes as normal and exercises strategies to manage stress • Seeks out trusted friends and adults to process stressors • Reasons through the relative significance of negative external influences • Attempts to identify the trigger for negative feelings • Considers other factors that may contribute to reactions to situations • Views challenges as opportunities to grow, instead of as tests of self-worth • Adopts a *task-involving* orientation, with a goal of mastering tasks, instead of an *ego-involving* orientation, with a goal of performing better than others	

There are other needs that may contribute to a student's lack of response to core instruction. While beyond the scope of this book, we will briefly describe three additional possible areas of deficit: English language, language and speech, and fine-motor skills.

English Language

English learners will require at least five years to be as proficient in English as their English-only peers. When English learners are not progressing at a rate consistent with their English learner peers who have been learning English for the same number of years, they may require supplemental English language supports. For example, English learners may require supplemental support if there is a difference between the number of years that the student has been learning English and that student's English language proficiency level—e.g., a student has been learning English for four years, yet has an English language proficiency level of two, as determined by mandated annual testing.

When a team determines that there may be delays in acquiring English, interventions in English language development may be appropriate. We also highly recommend that the team examine the quality and quantity of the English language development instruction that all students are receiving as part of core, Tier 1 instruction. Too often, the supports and scaffolds present in our day-to-day instruction are insufficient for English learners.

English language learners are students first. If students who are acquiring English are at risk, their *specific* needs must be met. For example, if English language learners seem to be developing their English skills at an appropriate rate (they have been learning English for two years and have an English language proficiency level of two) and yet are having difficulty reading, do not delay in providing supplemental supports in reading because of less-than-proficient but normally progressing abilities in English. While proficiency in reading and proficiency in English are related, we cannot delay intervening in a specific content, such as reading, simply because the student is still acquiring English and is doing so at an appropriate rate.

Likewise, if an English language learner is falling behind in reading, but the team determines that the reasons for the difficulties have more to do with delays in acquiring English than with challenges with phonics or comprehension, then a reading intervention rather than an English language intervention may not be appropriate. The point is this: we must be diagnostic in our assessments of student needs and targeted in our interventions. English language acquisition and reading have distinct characteristics and can be improved with distinct strategies.

Language and Speech

An inability to express, and perhaps to understand and process instruction and inputs, can negatively impact a student's success. There are many skills aside from speech articulation with which a speech and language pathologist can assist, such as these:

- *Phonological and auditory processing challenges*: Student errors resulting from difficulties organizing phonemes; e.g., producing a sound correctly but not using it appropriately; displaying a reduced sound inventory; or hearing sounds but not processing them correctly when segmenting or blending
- *Syntax challenges*: Student errors in constructing grammatically correct sentences and phrases
- *Semantic challenges*: Student errors in knowledge of word meaning or in knowing the difference between literal and figurative language
- *Pragmatic challenges*: Student errors in the use of language and behaviors in social contexts

When diagnosing student needs, we should consider the way that all students, not simply English language learners, are processing and using language. This is particularly relevant for elementary age students.

Fine-Motor Skills

Fine motor skills impact a critical function in school—writing. For example, a Kindergarten or first-grade student who has difficulties holding a pencil will have difficulty writing. This student will likely resist writing, and will likely write less than his or her classmates. Writing less will likely lead to less proficiency, competence, and confidence with writing. As with language and speech, this is particularly relevant for elementary age students. Teams may consider the presence of concerns within the following sets of skills:

- *Fine motor*: Moving the hands, wrists, and arms with dexterity, coordination, and strength
- *Visual-perceptual*: Using visual motor abilities and hand-eye coordination
- *Sensory-processing*: Receiving, organizing, and interpreting physical input

When a student is at risk we must consider any and all factors that may be contributing to difficulties, including deficits in academic skills, English language, behaviors, speech and language, and fine-motor development. Additionally, we must provide supports with a sense of urgency, with intensity, and with an expectation that students will respond to our supports.

There are many other types of valid assessments that we use throughout a school day and a school year. When we define "assessing" as "evidence-gathering," we can consider checks for understanding, weekly quizzes, students' collaborative conversations, and many other activities as assessments. The types of assessments described in this chapter highlight tests most common and critical in school that embrace the principles of RTI.

SCHOOL CULTURE

We will hear refrains and concerns in response to assessment, such as the following:

- **We just don't have time to assess.**

    As we suggested in this chapter, there are several tasks, beliefs, and practices to address the notion that we do not have time for assessments. First, inventory the assessments you are currently administering, using the tools provided in this chapter to ensure that we are gathering the timely information that we need to ensure that all students learn at high levels, but without redundancies and inefficiencies. Next, embrace the notion, and implement practices, that instruction and assessment are inextricably linked, and that checks for understanding and observations count and can inform instruction and grading. Finally, recognize that screening and pre-assessment, as is the case with other tests, can absolutely save time. Screening reveals students with such profound deficits that they will most certainly experience difficulties within the year, at some time and in some content area. Let's save time by initiating supports immediately. Pre-assessing prior to units will reveal students with gaps in their knowledge of immediate prerequisite skills, gaps that will likely necessitate interventions within the unit. Let's preteach prerequisites before and at the beginning of units to fill gaps, prepare students for success, and minimize the need to spend time later on interventions; moreover, pre-assessments can reveal that students already possess knowledge of content in upcoming units. By compacting content, we can avoid wasting time on content for which students already possess understanding, thereby allowing time for more depth of study or more practice with other content. We must have these conversations with staff who believe that there is not time for more assessment. And we must help staff with the practical steps required to inventory assessments, link instruction and assessments, and screen and pre-assess in a successful way.

- **It's not fair to allow students to retake assessments.**

    Some teachers express the belief that it is not fair to other students, students who passed the test the first time, when we allow multiple opportunities for students to take a test. Other teachers believe that we are not teaching responsibility when we allow multiple opportunities. And it is true: we have an important decision to make, because we simply cannot have both a firm commitment to all students learning at high levels and a firm commitment to only one chance to demonstrate that mastery. They are entirely incompatible. We all recognize, as parents, uncles, aunts, and/or teachers, that no two children learn at the same rate and in the same manner. To terminate instruction at an arbitrary date and suggest that learning of that content is at an end, and the one-time opportunity to demonstrate mastery is upon us, defies all logic. But, what about teaching responsibility? What are we teaching students when we communicate that they don't have to actually learn the content being assessed: Are we teaching that they are off the hook and need not keep trying? Does it not teach responsibility when we demand that students keep up with the new content *and* receive additional support on old content until they reach the level of understanding needed for them to be successful? We *are* teaching children—we are teaching them perseverance, to learn how to learn, and to continuously strive to improve. The "real world" for which we are preparing students is a myth. Colleges and universities increasingly embed multiple layers of supports for students. Careers have always provided multiple opportunities to enter the profession—multiple chances to pass the state teaching exam, multiple opportunities to pass the bar, multiple opportunities to revise the thesis or dissertation. It will not be easy and it will take collaborative action to design a system that provides remediation and allows for additional chances to take assessments. However, we cannot continue to defend a stance that denies the reality of the various ways and rates at which individuals learn. It is disingenuous, or worse, to craft mission statements that promise high levels of learning for all without the fine print that expresses that there are no second chances for the K–12 students we serve.

- **How many times do we allow students to retake a test to demonstrate mastery?**

    The simple answer is . . . as many times as it takes. In response to questions such as these, questions that almost seem rhetorical, we are inclined to ask the questioner, "What are the other options?" To give up, to dismiss the student from school, to break the news to parents that we cannot help their child learn?

    Our experiences have taught us, however, that we will almost never administer the same test repeatedly without success. We may, for example, recognize that students' difficulties with mastering the assessment reveal something to us about our instruction; adjusting instruction, even for one student, may make the difference. We may alternatively realize that the students *do* understand the concept and content, but cannot express their mastery in the form in which we assess. For example, an oral examination may need to replace the written. This is not to suggest that we will not hold the students and ourselves accountable for improved written expression, but if the learning target is related to identifying cause-and-effect in a story or analyzing the process of meiosis, the manner in which students meet the learning target is of secondary importance. Finally, a student's repeated inability to master a concept on a test may help us diagnose a more fundamental need, perhaps an auditory processing deficit or a challenge with short-term memory. Once discovered, we can support the student in this area, and subsequent instruction and assessment will result in more success.

- **What about grades?**

    There are two misunderstandings about assessment and grading within schools (Marzano, 2006). The first misunderstanding is that instruction is distinct from assessment. For example, "I taught the content for a week, and then I gave students a test." There is an unfortunate reluctance to assess students during the course of instruction, perhaps because teachers believe that they are unqualified to craft a valid assessment; they believe that informal evidence gathered during the course of instruction is unreliable and invalid to inform teaching and impossible to use when assigning grades. This is simply not the case. The second misunderstanding follows from the first: assessing for instruction and assessing for the purpose of determining a grade are distinct tasks. In fact, assessment *is* assessment, and the information gathered during assessments can be used for a variety of important purposes.

Grades should reflect what students learn, not how many points they earn. When schools use letter grades that include the number of points that students have accumulated completing homework, participating in class, or completing extra credit assignments, they are not measuring student mastery of prioritized standards. When students earn points, it is possible for students who do not adequately demonstrate mastery on assessments to pass a class. Alternatively, when students earn points, and possible points come from sources unrelated to mastery of standards, it is possible for students to fail a class even when they have mastered content by the end of the grading period.

Standards-based grading practices can exist; college-entrance requirements and high school transcripts do not make their use impossible. In fact, they are the only honest way of communicating student performance to stakeholders, including students and parents, in a transparent manner. It seems misleading to assign a D or F to a student who, despite earning 20 out of 100 points on the first assignment of the semester, earns 80 out of 100 on the next three assessments. However, given a traditional form of grading in which points are accumulated, this student would earn a 65 percent, which would be a D or lower in most schools. It seems equally misleading to give students a passing grade because they try hard and complete all their homework and we do not want to upset or anger parents. Instead, we should be communicating concerns early to parents and intervening within the semester with intensity, immediately on identifying the need.

We must start by discussing the purpose of grading, grades, and report cards in our schools. We believe that staffs will conclude that the purpose of grades is to communicate a student's current level of performance. We do not need to rely on averaged or calculated grades to validate this communication; we are professionals. We need to rely on evidence of student learning, evidence gathered from formal and informal assessments that we administer and analyze throughout a school year.

CHAPTER SUMMARY

CFAs and feedback significantly and positively improve student learning as much as any educational endeavor (Hattie, 2009). While we may have come to believe that we assess too much, we often face the challenge of helping students with an absence of necessary knowledge. Some call this condition DRIP—data rich, information poor.

To operationalize RTI, we must regularly screen to immediately identify students in need of intensive support; we must monitor progress to ensure that the supports we are providing, particularly supports to vulnerable students at risk, are appropriate; and we must diagnose to learn which supports will most successfully target student needs. We may not need more assessments, but we need to consider assessment differently. Without knowledge, we cannot meet the entirely realistic goal of high levels of learning for all students.

5

Tier 2 and 3 Interventions, Strategies, and Resources

When students are not responding to initial, core, Tier 1 instruction, the diagnostic interviews from Chapter 4 will shed light on the areas in which schools can first, and most accurately, provide supports. We strongly encourage teams to consider all possible causes of student difficulties (Figure 5.1).

In our experience, it is quite common for students to have needs in more than one area, and thus we strongly recommend that schools' problem-solving teams are prepared to provide supports in more than one area to best address student needs in the most expedient manner. Particularly as students at risk

Figure 5.1 Reasons Students Are at Risk

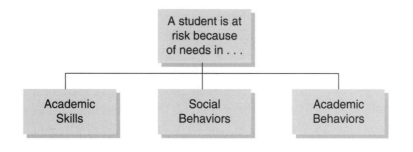

reach upper elementary grades, and for the remainder of their K–12 lives, it is unusual to find a student experiencing academic difficulties who does not have behaviors that inhibit learning. It is unusual to find a student whose misbehaviors are not, at least in part, caused by years of academic frustration. While we will define interventions, strategies, and resources in each area separately, we recognize that the most appropriate set of supports will involve integrated interventions from multiple areas.

In this chapter, we will present concrete strategies to use when intervening with students at risk in distinct areas. We recognize that students most at risk rarely have needs in only one area. Experience has taught us that deficits in one area can contribute to, or exacerbate, challenges in another area. Thus, we suggest that the reader ask these questions while progressing through this chapter:

- How would strategies and recommendations in one area potentially meet needs in another area?
- How could I combine more than one of these strategies or recommendations, even those in different content areas (e.g., phonics and comprehension, reading and behavior) to efficiently meet my students' needs?
- What is my overall goal when utilizing these strategies: not simply to improve phonics, but to increase student confidence and competence while interacting with text; not simply improving computation skills, but improving mathematics problem solving?

Given the quantity of practical research-based and evidence-based strategies that we provide in the area of academics and behavior, we will describe academic interventions in this chapter and behavioral supports in the next chapter.

ACADEMIC SKILLS

In the area of academic skill needs, there are two primary possibilities. The first possibility is that the student lacks sufficient proficiency with immediate prerequisite skills and thus requires a modest amount of remediation, including more time and differentiated supports with the prioritized standards of the grade level, course, or content area. This possibility was initially described by Bloom's Mastery Learning and is the domain of the teacher teams. The school should leverage all resources to provide these interventions, but the content of the supports will be closely related to the grade level, course, or content area's standards and skills. This level of academic support is often described as Tier 2.

Schools should build into schedules time during which teachers can give more support to students, and teams should use alternative approaches to ensure students' mastery of prioritized standards. If it's predictable, it's preventable. We can predict that there will be students for whom, either within or at the completion of a unit, we have evidence indicating they have not yet mastered prioritized standards. We must be prepared with time built into the school day that does not supplant initial instruction on prioritized content. We will discuss possible schedules and personnel for Tier 2 supports in Chapter 6. First, in Chapter 5, we will discuss the strategies and supports that may be most appropriate.

Whatever resources or strategies we use will never be as important as how we use them. There may be times when a purchased program is appropriate. This is not one of those times. The strategies and resources that will best meet student needs at Tier 2—more time and support with the prioritized academic standards and skills— will be identified by the grade level, course, or content area's teacher teams, using processes described in Chapter 3. Among the key questions that teams ask are these:

- Which standards or skills from the assessment require more attention?
- Which students did not master essential standards or skills?
- What patterns can we identify from student errors?
- Which instructional strategies proved to be most effective?

To a large extent, the expertise we need to meet student needs resides in our teams. When we appropriately create, administer, analyze, and utilize CFAs, Tier 2 supports can fluidly follow. Whether collaborating within schools or between schools, we will likely discover that one teacher has achieved relatively better results. Teams should seek out and identify the approaches or strategies that teachers with greater relative levels of success have utilized. The approaches and strategies identified will inform both Tier 2 and future Tier 1 instruction.

The second possibility is that the student's academic difficulties may require Tier 3 interventions. When students are not responding to Tier 2 supports, or when schools have screened to determine that students have gaps in foundational prerequisite skills, Tier 3 intensive academic interventions will be necessary. Moreover, schools will need to prepare scaffolds and accommodations so students can successfully access and demonstrate their mastery of Tier 1 prioritized standards within daily classroom instruction. When students are years behind their peers in reading, writing, mathematics, and English language acquisition, schools must bring all possible resources to bear—in other words, we must provide Tier 3 interventions.

There is one further critical note required before we turn to describing the types of supports that may be most appropriate in these areas. When a school identifies trends in the needs of students at risk, whether these needs are academic or behavioral, the quality and appropriateness of Tier 1 supports must be examined. We have found, for example, that when a large percentage of students are at risk in reading due to deficits in fluency, it is necessary for a school to examine core fluency content and instruction. Likewise, a large percentage of students at risk across content areas due to deficits in motivation may necessitate an examination of the engaging and differentiated qualities of core instruction.

READING INTERVENTIONS, STRATEGIES, AND RESOURCES

To be clear, the purpose of proficiencies in phonological awareness, phonics, fluency, and vocabulary, and even proficiency with comprehension skills and strategies, is so students can

- make meaning of text;
- extract useful knowledge from text;

- follow, process, and understand written language;
- practice intentional thinking in which meaning is constructed though interactions between text and reader;
- develop a lifelong love of reading; and
- read to learn and access new and varied information.

In other words, the purpose of all reading instruction is to build comprehension. We do not intervene in a domain of reading (e.g., phonics) because a student has scored low in that area, but because a deficit in this area will prevent that student from meeting those bulleted goals. This may seem like an unimportant distinction, but without a focus on the purpose of all reading instruction (or all writing, mathematics, English language, or behavior instruction), we focus on the trees instead of the forest.

In all areas, we recommend that diagnostic interviews determine the focus of interventions. The more informed and focused the interventions, the more successfully and quickly needs will be ameliorated. Thus, instead of providing general guided reading supports, schools should provide phonics interventions to address deficits in the area of phonics, or more diagnostically, should fill gaps in the specifically identified areas of phonics need. We strongly recommend that all staff at all levels have a working knowledge of reading and the characteristics of reading deficits (with the possible exception of phonological awareness for teachers in middle and high schools) so that students potentially at risk can be discovered and supported by all.

Phonological Awareness

Phonological awareness is an entirely oral skill—teachers orally prompt students and students orally respond. The ability to process sounds is a key prerequisite to the most common and efficient ways in which we learn to read (Adams, Foorman, Lundberg, & Beeler, 1998). Many of the same tasks that teachers and students practice under the banner of phonological awareness—isolating, identifying, comparing, segmenting, substituting, adding, deleting, blending—are also practiced in the domain of phonics. The difference between phonics and phonological awareness is that in phonics sounds are presented in the form of written words that students visually interpret. Nonetheless, when students experience difficulties distinguishing between sounds in words that are presented orally, it may portend a future difficulty with reading. With phonological awareness, the prescription should follow directly from the diagnosis. When a phonological awareness diagnostic interview reveals gaps, our first supports and interventions should directly address those identified gaps (needs). Table 5.1 provides common goal areas and an appropriate strategy to meet the need.

The broader umbrella of phonological awareness is most often found in classrooms within the narrower category of phonemic awareness; phonemic awareness is a subset of phonological awareness. Phonemes are the smallest units of sound within a language, and there are approximately forty-three phonemes in English. A student with difficulty processing sounds or phonemes will likely have some difficulty with oral tasks that focus on phonemes. We can predict that these students may have difficulty with the traditional

Table 5.1 Phonological Awareness Interventions

Goal Area	Strategy
Syllable discrimination	• Model and support students in "physically" identifying syllables in words through clapping or feeling the starts-stops-starts of vibrations in their throats and puffs of air from their mouths.
Rhyme	• Transition from syllables to onsets and rimes, modeling and supporting students in distinguishing similar rimes.
Phoneme identification	• Transition from onsets and rimes to phonemes, modeling and supporting students in distinguishing and segmenting phonemes, starting with the initial, then final, then medial sounds of CVC, CVCe, and CVVC words, before moving to CCVC, CVCC, and beyond.
Phoneme manipulation	• Transition from identification to manipulation of phonemes, modeling and supporting students in replacing initial, final, and medial phonemes in CVC, CVCe, and CVVC words, before moving to CCVC, CVCC, and beyond.

synthetic-phonics approach to teaching reading (described next) and may benefit from a more broadly phonological approach to introductory reading, including more practice with manipulating syllables, onsets, and rimes, in addition to phonemes. A working knowledge of phonological reading at this depth will assist all professionals and students.

Phonics

The purpose of all reading instruction is to help students make meaning of text, read to learn new material, and develop a lifelong love of reading. Phonics plays a role, and not only in early reading. A deep understanding of phonics allows students to decode unknown words and, when examining word parts (e.g., through morphological approaches), to make meaning of words. With phonics, as with phonological awareness, the prescription follows directly from the diagnosis. In other words, when a phonics diagnostic interview reveals gaps, our first supports and interventions should directly address those identified gaps (needs).

As was noted in the previous section, due to difficulties with auditory processing not all students will respond to phonetically based instruction. Similarly, not all students will respond to core instruction based on blending individual sounds. A working knowledge of phonics will allow teachers to consider other approaches to phonics, as defined by the National Reading Panel (National Institute of Child Health and Human Development, 2000):

- *Analogy phonics.* Teaching unfamiliar words by comparisons to known words
- *Analytic phonics.* Teaching to analyze letter–sound relations in previously learned words

- *Embedded phonics.* Teaching by embedding phonics instruction in text reading
- *Phonics through spelling.* Teaching to segment words into phonemes and to select letters for those phonemes
- *Synthetic phonics.* Teaching to convert letters into sounds and to blend sounds to form words

The message for schools and staffs when considering the most appropriate interventions for students in early reading is for them to consider alternative approaches for combining, blending, and attacking unknown words. No matter the core and supplemental supports that are deemed most appropriate, schools must ensure that instruction follows a systematic process. Table 5.2 identifies common goal areas and strategies that teachers could employ to achieve the goal.

Success with monosyllabic phonics does not ensure success with multisyllabic words. We have found that many of the readers at risk with whom we have worked in Grades 4 to 12 have difficulty attacking longer words. Skipping words or guessing the pronunciation of longer words affects fluency and comprehension. The bad news is that we too infrequently teach students to decode longer words. The good news is that there are simple and powerful strategies available to equip all students with a set of skills to attack words. The better news is that these same skills can provide students with strategies to make meaning of words.

Morphology and syllabication are strategies that positively impact decoding, fluency, meaning making (vocabulary), and comprehension. While a *phoneme* is the smallest unit of sound in a language, a *morpheme* is the smallest

Table 5.2 Phonics Interventions

Goal Area	Strategy
CVC	<ul><li>Model and support students in using synthetic phonics to blend words phoneme by phoneme.</li><li>Help students understand the purpose of phonics by engaging them in reading and writing activities that require them to apply the phonics information teachers have taught them (poetry is particularly effective).</li><li>Use manipulatives to help teach letter–sound relationships. These can include counters, sound boxes, and magnetic letters.</li><li>Use a developmental, differentiated spelling program such as *Words Their Way* so that students begin to recognize the patterns within words.</li></ul>
CVCe	<ul><li>Extend CVC supports to recognized patterns in which -Ce forms produce a long vowel sound.</li></ul>
Blends, digraphs, and diphthongs	<ul><li>Model and support students in attacking words by identifying onsets and rhymes.</li></ul>
Multisyllabic words	<ul><li>Model and support students in using syllabication (identifying the six syllable types) and morphology (identifying affixes and roots, inflected forms, free and bound morphemes) to both successfully pronounce and make meaning of words.</li></ul>

unit of meaning. Recognizing derivational and inflectional additions to roots not only helps students for whom longer words are intimidating when attacking words, but can also help students understand the meaning of words.

There are six syllable types, and, like morphology, knowledge of these types can assist students in pronouncing the words (words that they may have heard and words for which they may have a knowledge of meaning). Explicitly teaching students the six syllable types can provide the confidence and skills to read any word. A balanced approach to early phonics and a commitment to advanced phonics, particularly for students in upper elementary and secondary grades struggling with reading, is an essential form of working knowledge of reading that all staff must possess.

Fluency

Fluency instruction is critical and critically missing from Tier 1 instruction in too many classrooms. All students through at least sixth grade will benefit from explicit instruction and repeated daily practice in improving their rate, accuracy, and prosody. The idea is not to race through text, but rather to read more fluidly and naturally, so that the cognitive load of reciting text interferes as little as possible with making meaning of text. Students reciting words without attending to expression will not comprehend as successfully. The Tier 1 practice of fluency instruction need not take longer than ten minutes a day, with students working in homogenous or heterogeneous pairs. High rates of fluency, while not the be-all, end-all of reading, are highly correlated with improved comprehension (Hook & Jones, 2004; Mercer, Campbell, Miller, Mercer, & Lane, 2000, National Institute of Child Health and Human Development, 2000). Table 5.3 identifies some key goal areas in fluency intervention and a strategy that teachers could employ to achieve the goal.

When students are deemed to be at risk in reading and inadequate fluency is deemed to be a causal factor, intervention in fluency is essential and an excellent place to start. The reasons are significant:

- Materials are not costly.
- The skills needed on behalf of the interventionist are not substantial.

Table 5.3 Fluency Interventions

Goal Area	Strategy
Rate	• Ensure that students repeatedly read passages (three to five times) that lie within their independent or low-instructional range; easy reading makes reading easy.
Accuracy	• Consider slowing down a student's rate, reducing self-corrections and repeated words and phrases by modeling care and calmness when reading for greater meaning and understanding.
Prosody	• Model the use of chunking/scooping/phrasing and support students in employing this strategy to read with the same rhythm they use when speaking.

- Progress will likely be rapid, assuming that there are not phonics needs that are inhibiting access to text.
- Students' motivation and confidence is likely to increase with their reading rate and accuracy.

The formula for intervening in fluency is simple:

- Present students with practice text at their comfort level—easy reading makes reading easy.
- Model for students the technique of chunking, phrasing, or scooping to guide their practice in reading in a manner similar to the way in which they speak.
- Provide immediate, specific feedback to students and direct them to graph their progress.
- When students consistently reach a "cold" rate of reading at or above one hundred words correct per minute, "graduate" them to a reading level closer to their grade level.

Remember, our goal is not to create speed-readers, and adequate rates of fluency will not necessarily translate into students being able to read for meaning. If students are deficient in the area of fluency, then provide supplemental supports; if students are not deficient in fluency—in other words, if they read with a rate, accuracy, and prosody appropriate to their grade level—then focus on vocabulary and comprehension.

Vocabulary and Comprehension

Perhaps no single factor better predicts a student's comprehension of a text than extensive background knowledge (Hirsch, 2006; Stanovich, 1986, 1993). A robust and extensive vocabulary is equally important. And yet we face a conundrum: a student's vocabulary is best built by extensive and varied reading. However, a student for whom reading is challenging is unlikely to read extensively. Moreover, deficits in phonological awareness, phonics, fluency, and even comprehension skills and strategies are more efficiently ameliorated than gaps in vocabulary and background knowledge. This is practically significant because students at risk cannot afford to wait for weeks or months to begin to demonstrate rapid progress, and schools never have excess personnel and time to provide targeted reading intervention to students at risk in all five reading domains. To access text and read widely, students must have a background in phonological awareness, phonics, fluency, and the skills and strategies to make meaning. Through these skills, they will build vocabulary and a rich knowledge of varied content. We therefore recommend prioritizing precious and limited intervention resources on non-vocabulary domains.

We definitely recommend that schools examine the adequacy of their Tier 1 vocabulary instruction. Isabel Beck, Margaret McKeown, and Linda Kucan's "Bringing Words to Life" (2002) helps define the nature of the vocabulary challenge and the necessary additions to core instruction. Essentially, Beck and colleagues report that our instruction of Tier 1 (basic, high-frequency sight words) and Tier 3 (content-specific and text-specific words) vocabulary is typically adequate. However, we must improve our instruction of Tier 2 words—high-leverage academic vocabulary that students will encounter in multiple contents and contexts.

To organize the additions to core literacy instruction that are necessary in so many classrooms, we recommend a simple but proven method such as the strategies described by Robert Marzano and Deborah Pickering in *Building Academic Vocabulary: Teacher's Manual* (2005). Through vertical articulation, we recommend that staffs collaborate on the selection of approximately three Tier 2 words in each grade level that every student will study and master each week. Teachers should agree on a method and an organizer that all classrooms will employ to learn high-leverage academic vocabulary, so the manner by which students study words does not inhibit vocabulary acquisition. Vocabulary instruction is critical for improved comprehension as a skill (i.e., teaching vocabulary), and there is substantial room for improvement within core, Tier 1 instruction.

Reading deficits are the most common and most dire of difficulties that students can experience. Within the domain of reading difficulties, comprehension challenges without accompanying deficits in phonological awareness, phonics, or fluency are the most mysterious. What's happening, or not happening, in students' minds during reading? We next provide research-based and proven methods for meeting these types of student supports. It starts with a simple approach.

The legacies of *A Nation at Risk* (1983) and *No Child Left Behind* (2001) have been partially positive, but there have been undeniable deleterious effects as well. One of the most unfortunate has been the overwhelming number of standards and the sense that they are disconnected, both between content areas (e.g., cause and effect is a critical way of thinking in social studies, science, mathematics, and reading) and within content areas (e.g., place value and base-ten knowledge *must* be much more connected to computation). How does this relate to interventions in the area of reading comprehension? The big-box, English-language arts programs from major educational publishers commonly include more than thirty skills/strategies that schools teach and that students are expected to use when making meaning of text. For a student at risk in the area of reading, a new skill/strategy per week is completely overwhelming. Just as the student grasps the nature of the skill/strategy and its accompanying worksheet or graphic organizer, a new week brings a new story, a new skill/strategy, a new worksheet, and a new graphic organizer. Today's student would be forgiven for believing that the purpose of reading is to successfully employ a skill or strategy; it is instead, of course, to make meaning of text. Table 5.4 addresses this dilemma.

Students at risk in the area of comprehension will likely have been diagnosed to have difficulties in one or more of the four features in Table 5.4. Instead of comprehension intervention involving disjointed and unfocused reteaching of thirty or more skills/strategies, we recommend identifying the feature with which students require more support, and then addressing them through focused support on the feature, not on shallow knowledge of the skill.

Table 5.4   Organizing and Simplifying Comprehension Skills and Strategies

Address and utilize the following four processes . . .

Explicit		Implicit	
Organizing Text	**Structuring Text**	**Drawing Conclusions From Text**	**Interacting With Text**
• Compare and contrast elements. • Identify causes, events, and effects. • Describe characters. • Describe settings. • Describe plot. • Determine text organization. • Categorize and classify elements.	• Summarize story. • Identify the main idea or topic and details. • Sequence events. • Structure story through the beginning, middle, and end. • Identify the problem and solution. • Follow directions.	• Infer message. • Make connections between text and self. • Predict outcomes. • Evaluate story. • Draw conclusions. • Make generalizations. • Make judgments. • Make connections between texts. • Make connections between text and world.	• Visualize story. • Monitor/clarify phrase meaning. • Monitor/clarify word meaning. • Distinguish between fantasy and realism. • Distinguish between fact and opinion. • Determine the author's purpose. • Determine the author's viewpoint. • Identify propaganda. • Question text.

. . . to comprehend and make meaning.

Comprehension, making meaning of text, is the only reason we teach reading. The ways in which we too often equip students with skills and strategies to make sense of text does not meet the needs of students most at risk. We must be focused on specific reading skills when we intervene with students with deficits in reading comprehension. Most students are not deficient in all areas of reading (Valencia & Buly, 2005).

We are very much in favor of graphic organizers to make more concrete the very abstract notion of mentally organizing text and comprehension (Marzano et al., 2001). We do not advocate a new graphic organizer every week. Instead, we recommend a thoughtful, focused approach to making comprehension visual such as the organizers defined by Thinking Maps, Inc. Additionally, we recommend comprehension intervention that is focused on high-leverage, high-utility skills/strategies that are validated by research to best equip students with the tools to make meaning of text. Skills/strategies such as comparing/contrasting and summarizing should be the focus of the targeted supports we provide to students as they build their abilities to make meaning. In Table 5.4 we list the two most-high-leverage skills and strategies at the beginning of each column.

When repeatedly and successfully practiced with texts at their instructional level, students' abilities of comprehending text will improve. Table 5.5 provides intervention routines by which the high-leverage skills in Table 5.4 can be practiced.

Table 5.5   Vocabulary/Comprehension Interventions

Goal Area	Strategy
Vocabulary	• Acknowledge, underline, and record unknown words and use the context of the story or subject area. • Acknowledge, underline, and record unknown words and use morphology to make meaning. • Practice word attack skills and increase self-corrections until words "sound right."
Background knowledge	• Make resources (books, images, online) about current units of study available to students. • Design interdisciplinary units of study so that background knowledge from different content is mutually reinforced and so students struggling with background knowledge are not required to play "catch-up" in multiple areas. • Construct pictorial-input charts to illustrate key vocabulary and themes within a story or topic prior to beginning the unit of study: o Make these available and visible throughout the unit. • In small groups, preteach key vocabulary and themes to students at risk in background knowledge prior to the beginning of the unit.

Organizational features of text	• Practice recognizing predictable grammatical forms (and the functions they represent in English), e.g., comparatives and superlatives associated with compare and contrast; transition words and conjunctions associated with cause and effect.
	• Use graphic organizers to record the "organization" of the story or text:
	  o Double-bubble maps to compare and contrast characters
	  o Multiflow maps to illustrate the causes and effects of events
	  o Tree maps or divided circle maps to illustrate and label
	    1. Characters
	    2. Settings
	    3. Plots
	• Record the theme defined by these story elements in the center of the circle map or beneath the tree map.

Explicit interactions with text	• Practice recall and summarizing. • Write a sticky note that summarizes every paragraph. • Use graphic organizers to record details and synthesize to determine the main idea: o Use a circle map to record details; highlight common terms and topics; inductively construct the main idea in the center of the map.

(Continued)

Table 5.5 (Continued)

Goal Area	Strategy
	o Use a flow map to record and sequence events or topics throughout the text, by paragraph, column, or page. • Write the *gist* of the recorded sequence below the flow map to construct a summary.

Implicit conclusions from text	• Teach, model, and support students in using the "formula":
	
	o Inference = Experiences + Details
	    Experiences come from life, other texts, background knowledge
	    Details come from key words and key events within the text
	
	• Teach, model, and support students in stopping regularly (every sentence, paragraph, column, page) to mentally, orally, pictorially, or in writing
	
	o visualize the text,
	o connect the text to other text,
	o connect the text to life and experiences, and
	o connect the text to events in the world.

Implicit conclusions from text	• Pause to ask, "Does this make sense?" every sentence, paragraph, column, page. • Acknowledge, underline, and record unknown words and use the context of the story or subject area to make meaning. • Acknowledge, underline, and record unknown words and use morphology to make meaning. • On sticky notes or a separate piece of paper, maintain an ongoing dialogue with the text and author: o Why did the author choose to write this event or move the story in this direction? o For what purpose or lesson is the author writing this passage or story? o What is the meaning of this word, phrase or section?

All of these strategies and recommendations share a common goal: we are trying to increase and improve the ways in which students interact with text while reading. Whether identifying events, causes, and effects, or making text-to-self connections, we are simply attempting to improve students' comprehension of text through more frequent, successful, and meaningful interactions. Reading like a robot with no concern for meaning-making is unproductive; we must model and support students in becoming metacognitive readers.

Despite the risk of annoying by repetition, we state again: reading deficits are the most common and most dire of difficulties that students can experience. While thus far in this chapter we have explored reading needs as separate areas, we now draw on the important work of Valencia and Buly (2005) to conceptualize how to integrally support the most common readers at risk.

The Six Types of Readers At Risk

Just as prioritizing standards within a content area ensures a GVC that allows for learning for all at a level of depth and complexity heretofore rare in schools, we must also prioritize the manner in which we meet the needs of students at risk. Students with intensive needs, particularly in later grades, are likely to have deficits in multiple areas, e.g., reading, mathematics, behaviors, English language. We cannot adequately and intensively address them all simultaneously. Where do we start?

For students with intensive needs, we recommend that supports first be provided in the areas of behavior (both social and academic) and reading. These two areas not only represent areas of need of an overwhelming majority of students at risk and of students in special education, but they are also prerequisites in nearly every aspect of student life. Behavior supports will be discussed later in this chapter. Drawing on the work of Valencia and Buly (2005), we will describe the characteristics of six types of struggling readers and the strategies that teachers should consider for intervening with students displaying each type of deficit. Valencia and Buly studied the characteristics of students using multiple measures; none of these students had been determined eligible for special education services, yet they failed state-level reading assessments. Diagnoses, a topic of Chapter 4, and prescriptions are indelibly linked. The more accurate the diagnosis, the more successful the intervention, and the more rapid the success. Valencia and Buly describe six types of readers at risk (Table 5.6). Diagnosing students' reading difficulties using Valencia and Buly's framework can lead to the selection of the most appropriate, and successful, intervention strategies.

Despite its complexity, we must zealously and aggressively diagnose and meet student reading needs. The domain of fluency may be the wisest with which to begin. Particularly with older readers at risk, the relationship between fluency and comprehending is multifaceted. Students who do not understand words or passages should slow rate to monitor meaning, yet lack of automaticity and a slow rate may interfere with comprehension. We must read with students to determine the antecedents to difficulties and to determine appropriate supports. If fluency improves when readers at risk engage with text for which they possess background knowledge, the primary focus for intervention should likely be comprehension because disfluencies would seem to be the result of misunderstandings. If, however, fluency does not improve when readers at risk engage with text for which they possess background knowledge, instruction should focus on both fluency and comprehension. This example suggests that we must individualize diagnoses and supports. There are no perfect diagnostic assessments that we can purchase, and even Valencia and Buly's categories will not answer all our questions about students' reading needs. While the up-front time demands may be high, the goal is worthy. Reading is simply too important a skill to allow to languish at any grade level.

Table 5.6 Valencia and Buly Framework`

Type of Reading Difficulty	Characteristics of Students	Relative Strengths and Needs	Strategy Students . . . With Support From Teacher
Automatic Word Caller. Reads accurately and quickly; adequate vocabulary, but little comprehension.	• 18% of at risk readers • 63% EL • 89% low-SES	• Accurately reads words • Fluent • Poor comprehension	• Practice recall and summarizing. • Write a sticky note for every paragraph. • Create a mental picture for every sentence and paragraph. • Slow the rate, increase prosody. • Improve self-monitoring, help identify successful meaning-making skills. • Build vocabulary and background knowledge. • Acknowledge unknown words; use context and morphology to make meaning.
Struggling Word Caller. Reads at reasonable rate, but inaccurately; poor vocabulary and comprehension.	• 15% of at risk readers • 56% EL • 81% low-SES	• Significant number of errors when reading words • Fluent • Poor comprehension	• Practice with text closer to independent and low-instructional level. • Diagnose and meet phonics needs. • Slow rate, practice word-attack skills, and increase self-corrections until words "sound right." • Practice recognizing and producing predictable grammatical forms (and the functions they represent of English).
Word Stumbler. Numerous self-corrects and repeats impact fluency and accuracy; reads for meaning with adequate vocabulary.	• 17% of readers at risk • 16% EL • 42% low-SES	• Significant number of errors when reading • Disfluent • Moderate comprehension	• Diagnose and meet phonics needs, particularly multisyllabic word-attack skills. • Practice fluency through repeated reading and chunking/scooping/phrasing. • Access complex text through guided reading to build on comprehension strengths.

Type of Reading Difficulty	Characteristics of Students	Relative Strengths and Needs	Strategy Students . . . With Support From Teacher
Slow Comprehender. Reads accurately and for word-level and passage-level meaning; reads at a slow rate; does not read for pleasure.	• 24% of readers at risk • 19% EL • 54% low-SES	• Accurate reading of most words • Disfluent • Relatively good comprehension	• Practice fluency through repeated reading and chunking/scooping/phrasing. • Access complex text through guided reading to build on comprehension strengths. • Build stamina and endurance, pausing periodically to employ check-in strategies. • Select high-interest text.
Slow Word Caller. Reads accurately but disfluently; poor vocabulary; difficulty with explicit and implicit comprehension.	• 17% of readers at risk • 56% EL • 67% low-SES	• Accurate reading of most words • Disfluent • Poor comprehension	• Practice fluency through repeated reading and chunking/scooping/phrasing. • Practice recall and summarizing. • Write a sticky note for every paragraph. • Create a mental picture for every sentence and paragraph. • Build vocabulary and background knowledge. • Acknowledge unknown words; for example, use context and morphology to make meaning.
Disabled Reader. Reads inaccurately and disfluently; poor vocabulary and reading comprehension; adequate oral comprehension	• 9% of readers at risk • 20% EL • 80% low-SES	• Significant number of errors when reading words • Disfluent • Poor comprehension	• Diagnose and meet phonics needs. • Practice fluency through repeated reading and chunking/scooping/phrasing. • Access complex text through guided reading to build on comprehension strengths. • Practice recall and summarizing.

Source: Valencia & Buly (2005)

Note: EL = English language learners, SES = socio-economic status.

Valencia and Buly's gift to educators is simple and profound. When students are at risk in reading, we must intervene immediately and ameliorate gaps as quickly as possible. This necessitates a knowledge of *why* the student is experiencing difficulties, which will determine *what* supports we should initially provide. The more precise the diagnoses, the more targeted the supports, and the more rapidly the student will make gains.

Purchasing Reading Programs

Schools and educators frequently consider an important question: Should the school staff purchase, and should interventionists use, free, low-cost, and teacher-created materials, or should the school purchase commercially available intervention programs? Teachers possess the knowledge to select, craft, and teach interventions for students at risk. However, teachers have full-time jobs of some importance—they teach students. When do they have the time to design appropriately scoped and sequenced intervention programs? Moreover, classroom teachers are not always the staff members serving as interventionists. And while many interventionists are pedagogically sound educators, others may be newer teachers, paraprofessionals, or even volunteers. Well-designed and well-described lessons that are provided within commercially available programs, while they should be differentiated based on student need, provide a foundation for successful, differentiated intervention instruction. Successful schools, in which students close content gaps, often use high-quality, commercially available programs.

- Phonemic Awareness/Phonological Awareness
  - Early Reading Intervention (Scott Foresman)
  - Fast ForWord (Scientific Learning)

- Early Phonics
  - Read Well (Sopris Learning)

- Advanced Phonics
  - REWARDS (Sopris Learning)

- Fluency
  - Read Naturally
  - Six-Minute Solution (Sopris Learning)
  - Reading Assistant (Scientific Learning)

- Comprehension
  - Making Connections (EPS)
  - Reading Assistant (Scientific Learning)

Scaffolds and Accommodations to Access Core Content

Students' inabilities to read texts used in their current grade levels or courses will make accessing content and new learning challenging, for both students and teachers. However, reading difficulties must not prohibit students from learning. We must intervene to build the abilities of students who are currently reading below the level necessary to access grade-level tests, *and* we must scaffold new learning so the standards of the content area are accessible. This may require

- finding alternative texts that address content but are closer to the student's current reading levels, perhaps by matching Lexiles;
- using audio versions of the text or the course's prioritized content, perhaps prepared by the teacher and/or students during lessons; and
- using visual or video representations of the text or the course's prioritized content.

Scaffolding to ensure students can access information will be necessary within all subject areas, including scaffolding access to texts so students can practice comprehension in an English class. A student's inability to read at grade level for the purpose of practicing the use of skills, strategies, and techniques to make meaning of the written word is a concern that teachers must address through phonics and decoding supports. However, this inability cannot prevent students from accessing text; this *can* be completed with guidance and can be practiced with leveled texts.

WRITING INTERVENTIONS, STRATEGIES, AND RESOURCES

We rarely express concerns for a student's literacy deficits by concluding that the student simply cannot read. Instead, we further diagnose difficulties in reading. For example, students might have reading difficulties that seem to be partially caused by poor fluency, or more specifically, by poor rate and expression. Or students might have reading difficulties that seem to be partially caused by an inability to comprehend implicit ideas in a text, while recall of explicit details is sound, or vice versa. In the area of reading, we're prepared to dig deeper. We problem solve in this manner because we are attempting to identify the specific student needs that are preventing the student from making meaning through metacognitive interactions with text. We must be prepared to dig deeper and problem solve with a similar level of specificity in the domains of mathematics, behavior, and the topic of this section, writing.

The more targeted an intervention, the far more effective the intervention. The following areas of writing are based on the six traits of writing: (1) ideas, (2) organization, (3) voice, (4) word choice, (5) fluency, and (6) conventions. Deficits in fine motor skills can also negatively impact writing, particularly for younger students. Targeting these traits can ensure that supports for student writing are optimally effective.

Fine-Motor Skills

Students in primary grades in particular will be reluctant writers if the act of writing is painful or difficult for them. When holding a pencil to craft letters and numbers is laborious, and when the products of these efforts are illegible and result in less-than-positive reactions, writing is not enjoyable. When writing is not enjoyable, students are likely to produce less writing than their peers. And, when students produce less writing than their peers, their rate of improvement is not likely to be as robust.

When fine-motor challenges are inhibiting a student's writing, consider the strategies in Table 5.7.

Table 5.7 Writing Fine-Motor Strategies

Goal Area	Strategy
Strength and dexterity	• Students use their fingers to walk a ball up one leg, across the stomach and down the other leg. Students should start with the dominant hand. Ensure they use a walking motion and not a grabbing motion. • Students hold six to ten beans in a hand and place them into a container one at a time. Teachers can also reinforce number sense concepts such as counting and cardinality. • Students position their fingers under a beanbag, holding it horizontally, and then slowly rotate the beanbag 360 degrees with the fingers and thumb. • Students engage in structured play with connecting blocks, first with no rules but later creating multiblock shapes that match predesigned forms that increasingly challenge fine-motor skills. • Students serve as helpers by cleaning the classroom, squeezing water bottles, alternating hands to strengthen grips. Students can progress from four-finger to three-finger, to two-finger, and finally to one-finger grips. • Students serve as helpers, or just have fun, using hole punchers, alternating hands to strengthen grips. Students can progress from four-finger to three-finger, to two-finger, and finally to one-finger grips. • Students roll out, squeeze, and pound play dough; roll small balls; and create bowls and other objects using the palms of their hands and all five fingers. • Students push coins into piggy banks or money boxes, starting with one at a time and advancing to holding several coins in one hand and depositing them one by one. • Students create crepe paper "scrunchies" by crumpling small pieces of crepe paper with alternating hands using their fingers and thumbs. • Students practice isolating fingers for the tripod grip by placing their ring and little finger on an object while holding the middle finger, index finger, and thumb aloft. • Students grip a clothespin, with two dots on one side representing the middle and index fingers, and one dot on the other side representing the thumb. • Students use clothes pins to grasp small objects. • Students use the tripod fingers to hold a crayon horizontally and then rub the crayon over a piece of paper; square and triangular crayons are best. • Students use their index finger, middle finger, and thumb to tear strips, and then squares, of paper.

Goal Area	Strategy
Accuracy and legibility when writing symbols	• Students trace symbols on their paper or worksheet with their fingers prior to using a pencil. • Students trace symbols in sand, cornmeal, or with finger paints; the more textured and kinesthetic the feedback, the better. • Students write in the air with an outstretched hand. • Students examine and manipulate three-dimensional symbols when blindfolded. • Students use writing utensils to produce symbols with similar strokes, moving on to more-complex symbols before writing short combinations of symbols (words, multidigit numbers), that they can "read."

Ideas

We embrace writing as a fluid and organic act that can flourish in a workshop model. Our concerns lie with students for whom a workshop model is out of reach—students, for example, for whom recording thoughts on a blank page seems to be an overwhelming obstacle. If students have not produced any words, they can't learn how to revise and edit. When students have difficulty generating ideas about which they can construct sentences and paragraphs, consider the ideas in Table 5.8.

Table 5.8   Writing Ideas Strategies

Goal Area	Strategy
Prompt	• Students, initially with guidance, deconstruct a writing prompt and transform key ideas into the first sentence, topic sentences, and other key portions of pieces of writing using teacher-provided sentence frames and grammatical forms.
Main idea	• Students either discover or are provided with images and text related to the prompt or piece of writing, and add terms, phrases, and/or ideas to a bubble map. Initially with guidance, students highlight common and repeated ideas, synthesizing to craft a topic sentence using teacher-provided sentence frames and grammatical forms.
Details	• Building from a main idea or topic sentence, students talk through the writing with a teacher or peers recording their thoughts. Alternatively, students capture thoughts using a voice recorder for future playback; students use recorded thoughts to complete tree maps, adding details to various branches.

Organization

If students cannot express ideas logically and cogently, they will not be able to successfully communicate a narrative, opinion, or exposition. Identifying and providing students with scaffolds to represent the elements of a sentence and paragraph can guide the production of connected text. Targeting literary elements can further organize the totality of a piece of writing. When student writing includes rich ideas in an illogical sequence, consider the strategies in Table 5.9.

Table 5.9 Writing Organization Strategies

Goal Area	Strategy
Sentence formation	• Students produce complete sentences within a complete piece of writing using teacher-provided sentence frames and grammatical forms, with lesser amounts of provided words and more student-generated verbiage as their confidence and competence increases.
Paragraph and multiparagraph formation	• Students use a teacher-provided or class-created detailed tree map, in conjunction with teacher-provided sentence frames and grammatical forms to produce complete multisentence paragraphs and collections of multisentence paragraphs. • Students use teacher-provided or class-created color codes and numbering systems to organize and produce topic and concluding sentences, as well as the supporting sentences.
Literary elements	• Students use teacher-provided or class-created *who, what, where, when, how, why* templates, numbered paragraphs, and teacher-provided sentence frames and grammatical forms to produce complete, well-organized pieces of writing. • Students use teacher-provided or class-created *setting, characters, events* templates, numbered paragraphs, as well as teacher-provided sentence frames and grammatical forms to produce well-organized pieces of writing. • Students use teacher-provided or class-created *problem and solution* templates, numbered paragraphs, and teacher-provided sentence frames and grammatical forms to produce well-organized pieces of writing.

Voice, Word Choice, and Fluency

While perhaps not as severe an area of need as deficits in fine-motor skills or in the traits of ideas and organization, if student writing lacks voice, word choice, or fluency, the compelling nature of the narrative, argument, or exposition will lack power. These aspects of revision are likely a critical component of teacher's revision portion of the writing process or workshop. When students experience difficulties in revision, consider the strategies in Table 5.10.

Table 5.10 Writing Voice, Word Choice, and Fluency Strategies

Goal Area	Strategy
Voice	• Students open their piece with "Dear . . . ," and an opening line of "I'm writing this to . . . ," to emphasize the audience and purpose of the writing, no matter the genre of the piece (the student can later remove these openings). • Students create, or are provided with, images that represent the audience and purpose of the writing. • Students orally rehearse (read aloud) their prewriting or draft to a teacher, peer, or into a voice recorder to improve the extent to which their writing mirrors the *voice* with which they speak and orally tell stories.

Goal Area	Strategy

Word choice	• Teachers identify an area of focus, and during the revision phase of the writing process, students highlight the following:
	
	   ○ *Adjectives and adverbs.* Students reflect and consult with teachers and peers to choose more-precise and descriptive adjectives and adverbs.
	   ○ *Similes and metaphors.* Students reflect and consult with teachers and peers to find locations within their writing where similes and metaphors might be appropriate, and then construct these devices.

Fluency	• Students orally rehearse (read aloud) their prewriting or draft to a teacher, peer, or into a voice recorder to improve the extent to which their writing mirrors the *fluency* with which they speak and orally tell stories.
	• Teachers identify an area of focus, and during the revision phase of the writing process, students highlight the following:
	
	   ○ *Nouns and pronouns.* Students reflect and consult with teachers and peers to find nouns and pronouns within their writing, and adjust the use of nouns or pronouns to vary the flow of the piece and ensure precision. ("Is it clear what you are referring to here?")
	   ○ *Sentence types.* Students reflect and consult with teachers and peers to label the types of sentences (simple, compound, complex, complex begun with appositives) within their writing, and adjust the use of sentence types to vary the flow of the piece and ensure precision. ("Let's stop when this sounds dull or repetitive.")

Conventions

Writing with compromised grammar, mechanics, punctuation, or spelling fails to accurately communicate, and may even embarrass the writer in the reader's eyes. Editing, like revision, is a critical component of classroom's writing process or workshop. When students do not correctly, competently, and consistently employ conventions, or when their core instruction is inadequate, consider the strategies in Table 5.11.

Purchasing Writing Programs

Teachers can, given time, design writing interventions for students for whom the prewriting, drafting, revision, and/or editing phases of the writing process prove to be difficult. Just as in reading, however, teachers are busy designing engaging and differentiated core writing experiences. We have had positive experiences with the following writing programs:

- Write from the Beginning and Beyond (Thinking Maps)
- Step Up to Writing® (Sopris Learning)

Scaffolds and Accommodations to Access Core Content

Students who cannot *read* at a level adequate to comprehend the core texts of the grade level and content area will not be able to *access* knowledge in the absence of the strategies described in Tables 5.7 through 5.11. We must both

Table 5.11 Writing Conventions Strategies

Teachers identify an area of focus during the "editing" phase of the writing process and students highlight:

Goal Area	Strategy
Sentence structure, punctuation, spelling, and other conventions	• *Subject-verb and other agreements.* After highlighting subjects and verbs within their writing, students consult teacher-provided guides, classroom resources, and authentic text to evaluate whether each of their sentences attain agreement.
	• *Punctuation.* After highlighting the predetermined punctuation marks within their writing, students consult teacher-provided guides, classroom resources, and authentic text to evaluate whether they have used the appropriate ending punctuation, commas, apostrophes, colons, and/or semicolons. Students then look at any "unhighlighted" portions of the piece of writing in which some form of punctuation might be necessary.
	• *Spelling.* After highlighting words that look "fishy" within their writing, students consult with peers and their *Words Their Way* (or other spelling) journals to evaluate whether the words match known patterns; alternatively, students type and then use spell check to edit their spelling, recording their errors and corrections on a teacher-provided form.

provide reading interventions and identify and employ other ways of ensuring students can learn new material.

Students who cannot *write* at a level adequate to the demands of the grade level and content area will not be able to *demonstrate* their understanding or to show what they have learned in the absence of scaffolds. Students may very well have mastered new content and challenges and yet be unable to show us what they know. As a temporary scaffold while we also intervene to improve their ability to communicate in writing, we must identify and employ other ways for students to show what they know, such as

- oral assessments;
- graphic organizers, which involve fewer writing demands, including the option to use phrases and words instead of complete sentences and paragraphs;
- graphical representations including drawings, Microsoft PowerPoint, and Kid Pix that allow for the use of clip art and other visuals; and
- peer or group projects, in which all students are responsible for content knowledge, but one takes the lead on writing and others take the lead on oral presentations, computations, figures, or collating the final product.

MATHEMATICS INTERVENTIONS, STRATEGIES, AND RESOURCES

Algebra is a civil right. Through an examination of skills most essential for success in algebra, educators can gain practical and useful guidance for determining the essential, foundational prerequisite skills on which teachers should devote the most focus when intervening. Algebra is critically important to high school success and postsecondary and career readiness. While Tier 3 supports in any content or domain should focus on those antecedent, foundational skills with which students are diagnosed to have difficulties, we have found that there is often a correlation between these diagnosed areas and the essential prerequisites of algebra:

- Early numeracy, number sense, and computation strategies
- Fractional awareness and proportional reasoning
- Word problems

Early Numeracy, Number Sense, and Computation Strategies

The concept of number sense permeates all other strands of mathematics and should be a focus throughout the year (Gersten, Clarke, Haymond, & Jordan, 2011, Wurman & Wilson, 2012). Number sense allows students to understand the meaning of numbers, decompose numbers, develop strategies for solving complex problems, make simple magnitude comparisons, create procedures for performing operations, and recognize appropriate estimates and inappropriate errors. A sense of number represents "the presence of powerful organizing schemata that we refer to as central conceptual structures" (Kalchman, Moss, & Case, 2001, p. 2). Number sense is critical to developing proficiency with mathematical procedures and understanding mathematical concepts. A sense of number helps students develop a mental number line and mental mathematical images, and it allows them to represent and manipulate quantities and solve a variety of mathematical problems.

Lack of number sense may contribute to learning difficulties and disabilities (Gersten & Chard, 1999). Explicit instruction in number sense reduces failure in early mathematics and integrating number sense with computational fluency instruction benefits all students. In this way, number sense is analogous to phonemic awareness and phonics. Just as phonemic awareness and phonics are necessary for fluent reading and ultimately reading comprehension, number sense provides the foundation for other mathematics. Number sense instruction has the potential to help students build both computational fluency and problem-solving skills (Gersten & Chard, 1999).

Conceptual and procedural competencies with number sense are fundamentally important to students—as important as reading accurately, fluently, and for meaning. One key to number sense, as emphasized in next-generation standards, is a deep understanding of place value and the base-ten number system; this understanding must be deep enough to be used in computation, including multidigit computation, and thorough enough to serve as a foundation for algebraic thinking. The expectation for computational fluency with single digits and within one hundred are equally robust—students must not simply know math facts fluently, they must know them with automaticity. A student who "sounds out" CVC words in a reasonable amount of time may have fluency, but we expect these words to quickly become sight words. When presented with "cat" or "fog," we expect students to read these words automatically, without applying phonics. The same must be true for math facts; students must know facts by "sight," with automaticity, and they must know them before they leave third grade to explore and master the mathematics that follows. A true sense of number will facilitate this automaticity and future success. The strategies in Table 5.12 will serve all students, particularly those for whom number sense has proven challenging, and must be modeled so that students understand and apply these concepts and procedures:

Table 5.12 Early Numeracy, Number Sense, and Computation Strategies

Goal Area	Strategy
Early numeracy	• *Concrete-representational-abstract* (CRA). We must introduce and practice all mathematics concepts in three ways—concretely, representationally (or pictorially), and abstractly. For example, when building 14, students first manipulate rods (a 3D or concrete activity) and cubes, eventually exchanging 10 "cubes" for 1 rod; next, students use 10 blocks drawn on worksheets (or 2 10-frames) to build and represent 14 (a 2D or representational activity); finally, students represent 14 using the digit "1" in the 10s place and the digit "4" in the 1s place (the symbolic or abstract depiction of 14). • *Visual-auditory-kinesthetic.* We must, whenever possible, communicate and practice all mathematics concepts in 3 ways. First visually: show students 1 cube at a time until 14 cubes are present. Second, combine this visual with auditory reinforcement, verbally counting by 1 as each cube is added. Finally, involve a physical movement: students move an arm down for each added cube, and/ or students hold up 1 finger for each added cube, bringing both arms and hands down when 10 is reached before proceeding. • *Hundreds chart.* There are an infinite number of uses for the Hundreds Chart for helping students visualize number, counting, patterns, and the base-10 system. • *Cubes, rods, and flats.* In either their 3D or 2D form, cubes, rods, and flats can assist in counting, cardinality, correspondence, and conservation, and can also facilitate a conceptual understanding of addition and subtraction, including regrouping. • *Varied visual arrangements of numbers.* Display a number in a variety of formats (e.g., 6 can be with 3 × 2 dots, or 2 × 3 dots, or 1 × 6 dots, or with 3, 2, 1 dot pyramid); an effective strategy for conservation and a preview of decomposition. Ask students to describe the pattern (they'll catch on quickly) and ask them to pick a favorite pattern and describe why, which leads to . . .

Goal Area	Strategy
Early numeracy *(continued)*	• *Metacognition.* We must, always, model the ways in which we think about our thinking of mathematics (and any other task). Number sense is an absolute prerequisite of mathematics, but students need not, and will not, make sense of number in the same way. Allow them to describe their understanding, validating it when correct, celebrating it when unique, and correcting it quickly and respectfully when students are mistaken.
Number sense	• *Decomposition.* Decomposition (the number 8 can be represented concretely, representationally, or abstractly as 5 + 3, 1 + 7, even 10 − 2) is critical to developing a sense of number, and will greatly contribute to a conceptual and procedural understanding of computation with all four operations. • *Expanded form.* The importance of expanded form, like decomposition, cannot be overstated. While we "taught" expanded form, we too rarely made explicit connections from the expanded forms of numbers to place value and to computation with all 4 operations. We will detail the ways in which expanded form can contribute to computation within the computation strategies section of this table; we must start by using expanded form to help students make sense of numbers, particularly with the base-10 nature of numbers. • *Estimation.* Estimation is a very practical application of rounding; in addition, a more liberal application of estimation will ensure students can make sense of numbers—whole numbers, decimals (to the nearest anchor decimals, e.g., 0.25, 0.5, 0.75) and fractions (to the nearest anchor fractions, e.g., $\frac{1}{4}, \frac{1}{2}, \frac{3}{4}$). Evaluating the reasonableness of results is a critical 21st century skill. • *Mental math.* Explicit, guided practice with mental math can increase students' competence and confidence with computation, but it can also build number sense. Teachers should model the different strategies they use when mentally computing a string of numbers and operations (e.g., start with 20, cut it in half, multiply by 3, subtract 5; start with the number of centimeters in a meter, double it, divide by the number of sides in a pentagon). Then teachers should explain how they solved each successive operation, followed by students participating and communicating their perhaps unique approaches to additional computation strings, validating them when correct, celebrating them when unique, and correcting quickly and respectfully when students are mistaken.
Computation strategies: Addition and subtraction	• *Hundreds Chart.* Once CRA methods of modeling addition and subtraction are practiced, the Hundreds Chart is a helpful and sound scaffold for students; it can, in fact, serve as a representational approach to addition and subtraction. The base-10 number system can be demonstrated by moving vertically and horizontally.

(Continued)

Table 5.12 (Continued)

Goal Area	Strategy
Computation strategies: Addition and subtraction *(continued)*	• *Addition with the expanded form and associative property.* By rewriting numbers in their expanded forms and then reordering which numbers are added to which numbers, students gain a more conceptual understanding of addition and benefit from a smoother transition to column addition with regrouping, e.g., 452 + 868 = (400 + 50 + 2) + (800 + 60 + 8) = (400 + 800) + (50 + 60) + (2 + 8) • *Subtraction with decomposition and the branch method.* By strategically decomposing numbers to create "branches" that will subtract without regrouping, once the associative property is applied, students gain a more conceptual understanding of subtraction and benefit from a smoother transition to column subtraction with regrouping, e.g., 72 − 36 = (60 +12) − (30 + 6) = (60 − 30) + (12 − 6) • *Cover, copy, and compare.* The cover, copy, and compare strategy works in many content areas, allowing students to take responsibility for their own learning, and can be applied to any problem with which they have had difficulty, including addition, subtraction, multiplication, and division.
Computation strategies: Multiplication and division	• *Times tables.* The times table can do for multiplication and division what the Hundreds Chart can do for addition and subtraction. With modeling, students can discover and articulate patterns (horizontally and vertically), build off existing knowledge ("I know 3 × 6 = 18 . . . where would I look for 4 × 6 . . . or 3 × 7?"), and connect division and multiplication ("To find 48 ÷ 8, I can start with 8 and . . ."). • *Area models.* After rewriting factors in expanded form, students use grid paper to accurately represent one expanded factor horizontally and the other vertically, creating a large rectangle with multiple smaller rectangles. Easier products can then be computed (or squares can be counted) and then the sum of the factors can be found. In addition to a useful scaffold, students gain a more conceptual understanding of multiplication and benefit from a smoother transition to the multidigit multiplication procedure. In addition to many other benefits, proficiency with the area model will provide a foundation for measurement, the distributive property, and algebra. • *Decomposition and distributive property.* Alternatively, factors can be more creatively decomposed and the distributive property can be employed. For example, to find 5 × 12, students could decompose 12 into 10 and 2, creating 5 × (10 + 2). Use of the distributive property will result in (5 × 10) + (5 × 2), computations with which students will likely have more success. • *Partial quotient.* Long division is certainly not the only method of finding multidigit quotients. Building off the notion of repeated subtraction (an excellent alternative to long division, but impractical for larger dividends with smaller divisors), students identify a more even number of multiples that will divide into the dividend, and then

Goal Area	Strategy
Computation strategies: Multiplication and division *(continued)*	subtract and repeat the process. For example, given the problem 504 ÷ 24, students may recognize that there are at least 10 "24s" in 504, recording "10" to the side under a column titled "quotient" and subtracting 240 from 504, leaving 264. Students may then recognize that there at another 10 "24s" in 264, recording "10" to the side under a column titled "quotient" and subtracting 240 from 264, leaving 24. Students would then recognize that there is "24" remaining, write a "1" in the "quotient" column and adding the partial quotients to arrive at the final quotient, 21. • *Division by decomposing the dividend.* Students can decompose 504 into (240 + 240 + 24), then divide the divisor into each partial dividend, completing the problem using the partial quotient process in the bullet above.

Fractional Awareness and Proportional Reasoning

Why plan on intervening with fractions? The most obvious answer is that students have a fear of fractions that is only matched by their fear of word problems; this fear is coupled with a significant lack of proficiency in understanding and computing with fractions. However, this answer cannot discourage teachers or students in their commitment to persevere with fractions; fractional awareness is a prerequisite to success in algebra. What about fractions makes them essential to later mathematics?

- Fractions are a way we represent numbers between zero and one.
- Fractions and fractional notation are key to defining rational numbers, and can be interpreted and represented as division problems, allowing us to construct decimals.
- Fractional notation is the format that we use to represent ratios and unit rates when performing computations; among other applications, unit rates provide the foundation for the slope of a line.
- Fractions, as ratios, provide the foundation for proportional reasoning.

This last statement may be the reason of most long-lasting importance. Through the proportional equation $\frac{a}{b} = \frac{c}{d}$ (where a, b, c, and d are integers that may or may not be different), problems of an impressive variety can be solved, including finding

- equivalent fractions,
- percents,
- percents of change and error, and
- simple interest, tax, markups and markdowns, gratuities and commissions, and fees.

In addition, and more simply, fraction awareness is a key component of number sense, and competency with fractional computation is a key to problem solving within algebra and beyond.

The strategies in Table 5.13 will help all students, particularly students at risk, gain greater conceptual and procedural knowledge of fractions, computation with fractions, and proportional reasoning. Each must be modeled by teachers and consistently used in classroom problem solving; in addition, teachers must hold students accountable to employing them in their critical thinking and their rustications of solutions.

Table 5.13   Fractional Awareness and Proportional Reasoning Strategies

Goal Area	Strategy

Fractional awareness	• *Area models.* Representing fractions using rectangles, supported by grid paper, serves both short-term and long-term needs. In the short term, students can visualize fractions such as $\frac{1}{2}$, $\frac{2}{5}$, or $\frac{1}{6}$. Fractions can and should be represented with rectangles of various dimensions. For example, $\frac{1}{6}$ can be represented with a 2×3, 3×2, 6×1, or 1×6 rectangle, with 1 "unit square" of the rectangle shaded. In the long term, these visual area models can support both a conceptual understanding and procedural fluency with finding equivalent fractions and performing all 4 operations with fractions.
	• *Fractions on a number line.* It is equally important to represent fractions on a number line segment that spans from 0 to 1, initially segmented with a number of tics that match the fraction's denominator.
	• Ensure that students understand that the fraction bar (the "vinculum"—also the name of the division "house") represents division. Through division, we can construct decimals that are equivalent to the fractions that create them.
	• *Partitioning.* To complement and supplement the use of area models, teachers and students should comfortably use
	  ○ shaded portions of arrays;
	  ○ shaded portions of equally sized parts of a compound figure; and
	  ○ shaded portions of equally sized objects in a set—circles, line segments, and nontraditional polygons to visualize fractions and, with area models, to compare and order.
	• *Hundreds grid.* Rods and flats (representations of 10- and 100-unit squares) can be used to represent fractions with denominators of 10 and 100 and to model decimals.
	• *Unitizing.* Unitizing is defined as the assignment of a unit of measure to a given quantity or "chunk" that makes up a given quantity (Lamon, 2007). For example, the image could represent 7 (shaded circles), or $3\frac{1}{2}$ (columns), or $\frac{7}{12}$ (of a dozen), $1\frac{3}{4}$ (bundles of 4), or $1\frac{1}{6}$ (bundles of 6 or rows) depending on what "chunk" or unit you use as the reference whole or unit. All of these answers can be argued as correct, and for each the unit (or chunk) is different. Practice and proficiency with unitizing will greatly enhance students' fractional number sense.

Goal Area	Strategy

Proportional reasoning	• *The proportion equation.* The proportion equation is critically important and unbelievably practical. Used strategically, it can serve as a tool to solve dozens of mathematics problems. The equation $\frac{a}{b} = \frac{c}{d}$ serves as a foundation for proportional reasoning, starting with identifying and finding equivalent fractions, and then when adding and subtracting fractions with unlike denominators. When solving for a term of the proportion equation, teachers and students should first attempt to solve by "inspection." The number sense behind proportional reasoning is symbolized by the equal sign. Teachers should allow students to reason through the solution. When solving algebraically, teachers should first show students *why* "cross-multiply and divide" works before employing this useful strategy. For example, when solving $\frac{2}{3} = \frac{8}{x}$, first talk with students about "clearing denominators," a strategy that will serve students throughout the mathematics career: $\frac{3}{1} \cdot \frac{2}{3} = \frac{8}{x} \cdot \frac{3}{1}$ multiplying both sides of the equation by $\frac{3}{1}$, the reciprocal of the first ratio's denominator. Next, multiply $\frac{x}{1} \cdot \frac{2}{1} = \frac{24}{x} \cdot \frac{x}{1}$, multiplying both sides of the equation by $\frac{x}{1}$, the reciprocal of the second ratio's denominator, leaving the simple equation, $2x = 24$. Once students understand the concept behind "cross-multiply and divide," they can employ this strategy. Teachers should regularly ask them to explain how this strategy works orally or in writing.
	
	   The proportion equation can be used to solve many other types of problems when students restate questions, as part of the planning process, using the frame: What is ___% of ____? and the proportion, $\frac{is}{of} = \frac{\%}{100}$. For example,
	
	 o Harvey has \$50 in a savings account. The interest rate is 8% per year. How much interest will he earn in a year?
	
	   "What is 8% of 50?"
	
	   $\frac{x}{50} = \frac{8}{100}$ and multiplying by time, in number of years.
	
	 o The original price of a computer printer is \$80. Which coupon is a better deal? 25% off or \$25 off?
	
	   "What is 25% of 80?"
	
	   $\frac{x}{80} = \frac{25}{100}$, before completing the problem.
	
	 o Due to the popularity of tickets to the concert, the ticket agency marked up the cost of the tickets by 40%. Chelsea bought a ticket that originally cost \$40. What did Chelsea pay after adding the mark-up?
	
	   $\frac{x}{40} = \frac{40}{100}$, before completing the problem.

(Continued)

Table 5.13 (Continued)

Goal Area	Strategy
Proportional reasoning *(continued)*	○ The accountant charges a fee of 12% of every dollar of income on tax returns. Chip had $80,000 of income on his tax return. How much does he owe his accountant? "What is 12% of $80,000?" $\dfrac{x}{80,000} = \dfrac{12}{100}$, before completing the problem. ○ Janice was lucky to find a new $60 jacket for 30% off. What was the final price that Janice paid? "What is 30% of $60?" $\dfrac{x}{60} = \dfrac{30}{100}$, before completing the problem. ○ Bobby scored a 14 on his first test and a 21 on his second test. What was the percent change in his performance? Was it a percent increase or decrease? "7 (the increase) is what percent of 14 (the first test score)?" $\dfrac{7}{14} = \dfrac{x}{100}$, before completing the problem. ○ Students measured 45 mL of water in the beaker. The exact amount of water in the beaker was 40 mL. What is the percent error? "5 (the difference) is what percent of 40 (the measured amount)?" $\dfrac{5}{40} = \dfrac{x}{100}$, before completing the problem. There are, of course, other methods that we can use to solve these problems. Use them. Celebrate when students use other methods successfully. When working with students, however, particularly students at risk in mathematics, employing a consistent strategy is beneficial. The proportion equation is sound conceptually and can be leveraged to solve many types of problems.
Fraction-decimal-percent	• A key to number sense is knowing that a number can be equivalently expressed as a fraction, decimal, and percent. Students must understand this phenomenon and fluently convert between the three different representations. For example, ○ Convert $\dfrac{3}{4}$ into a decimal. $$3 \div 4 =$$ ○ Convert 0.75 into a fraction. $$\dfrac{75}{100} =$$ ○ Convert 0.75 into a percent. $$\dfrac{75}{100} = \dfrac{x}{100}$$

Goal Area	Strategy
Fraction-decimal-percent *(continued)*	○ Convert $\frac{3}{4}$ into a percent. $$\frac{3}{4}=\frac{x}{100}$$ ○ Convert 75% into a decimal. $$75\div100=$$ ○ Convert 75% into a fraction. $$\frac{75}{100}=$$
Adding and subtracting fractions	• *Common denominators* (*not LCD*). Least common denominators (LCD) are not necessary to add and subtract fractions. Instead, guide students to find equivalent fractions that have the same denominator. Simplifying or reducing the sum or difference may be necessary, but that's just another opportunity to find equivalent fractions. To help students visualize addition of fractions, use . . . • *Visual models.* Use grid paper to construct visual models of fractions to add and subtract. For example, to add $\frac{1}{3}+\frac{1}{2}$ Each fraction should have the same "length" and "width." Each unit can be further segmented if necessary. Students should be able to "see" that the numerators (shaded areas) cannot be added because denominators (the size of each figure's rectangular units) are not the same size. How can we make them the same size? Students can "see" that they can create equivalently shaded figures by segmenting both figures into sixths: Now, equally sized units can be added, yielding

Table 5.13 (Continued)

Goal Area	Strategy
Adding and subtracting fractions *(continued)*	As a fraction's denominators become larger, rectangles with other dimensions can be used. For example, to subtract $\frac{3}{4} - \frac{1}{6}$ Students should be able to "see" that be numerators (shaded areas) cannot be subtracted because denominators (the size of each figure's rectangular units) are not the same size. How can we make them the same size? Students can "see" that they can create equivalently shaded figures by segmenting each unit of the first model into thirds and each of the second unit in half:

Goal Area	Strategy
Adding and subtracting fractions *(continued)*	Now, equally sized units can be subtracted, yielding Visual models can also be used to help students "see" why and how to convert from improper fractions to mixed numbers, or from mixed numbers to improper fractions.
Multiplying and dividing	• *Fractions as operators.* A strategy for helping students conceptualize multiplication of whole numbers by fractions (or the division of whole numbers by fractions after taking the reciprocal of the divisor), and a strategy that will likely lead to more successful answers, is to split the multiplication into two operators: first, multiply by the numerator, then divide by the denominator. For example, $9 \cdot \frac{2}{3} =$ would be understood as $9 \cdot 2 = 18$ and $18 \div 3 = 6$. • *Mixed numbers using the distributive property.* A strategy for helping students conceptualize multiplication of whole numbers, fractions, or mixed numbers by mixed numbers (or division after taking the reciprocal of the divisor), and a

Table 5.13 (Continued)

Goal Area	Strategy
Multiplying and dividing *(continued)*	strategy that will likely lead to more successful answers, is to use the distributive property. For example, $1\frac{7}{8} \cdot 3\frac{1}{3} = \left(1 + \frac{7}{8}\right) \cdot \left(3 + \frac{1}{3}\right) = (1 \cdot 3) + \left(1 \cdot \frac{1}{3}\right) + \left(\frac{7}{8} \cdot 3\right) + \left(\frac{7}{8} \cdot \frac{1}{3}\right)$. Solving problems in this manner will take more time, so we would not recommend that all instances in which mixed numbers are multiplied and divided be completed using the distributive property. However, students may be able to conceptualize the solution process to a greater extent, and while they will compute four products instead of one, each product may be simpler and will likely make more sense. • *Visual models.* As with addition and subtraction, visual models for multiplication and division can benefit all students, particularly students for whom mathematics presents a challenge, in both conceptual understanding and in more consistently arriving at correct solutions. • For example, $\frac{2}{3} \cdot \frac{1}{4} =$ could be modeled with the following visual: $\frac{2}{3}$ times $\frac{1}{4}$: yields $\frac{2}{12}$ or $\frac{1}{6}$ of the units shaded.

Goal Area	Strategy
Multiplying and dividing *(continued)*	The division problem, $\frac{2}{3} \div \frac{1}{4} =$, could be modeled two ways. First, students could find the reciprocal of the divisor and solve the problem, $\frac{2}{3} \cdot \frac{4}{1} =$, which could be modeled as

+

+

+

which would yield an answer of $\frac{8}{3}$ or,

Table 5.13 (Continued)

Goal Area	Strategy
Multiplying and dividing *(continued)*	The second method, and perhaps the method that makes more conceptual sense, is to "divide" $\frac{2}{3}$ into fourths ("How many fourths are in two-thirds?"): $\frac{2}{3}$ $\div \frac{1}{4}$ yields or $2\frac{2}{3}$

Word Problems

Students' difficulties with word problems, and the need for explicit instruction and intervention with word problems, is referenced throughout the final report of the National Mathematics Advisory Panel (2008). We propose, based on evidence (National Research Council, 2001) and our experiences, that students' difficulties are due to two factors:

1. Students have not received consistent, widely applicable strategies for problem solving and solving word problems.

2. Teachers and students have not practiced sufficiently with word problems.

Both factors must change. The strategies in Table 5.14 can equip students with the tools to persevere through the process of solving real-world and word problems:

Table 5.14   Word Problem Strategies

Strategies

- *Bar model.* Explicitly teach students the bar model. It can be used to solve a multitude of mathematics problems from Kindergarten through high school. In the bar model, bars are used to represent quantities, with the bar split to represent parts of the whole (Ginsburg et al., 2005).

  o 122 girls and 95 boys went on the field trip. How many students went on the field trip?
    Two parts are given. To find the whole, add 122 and 95.

122 girls	95 boys
? students	

  o 217 students went on the field trip. There were 122 girls on the trip. How many boys were on the trip?
    The whole and one part are given. To find the missing part, subtract 122 from 217.

217 students	
122 girls	? boys

  o 95 boys went on the field trip. 42 more girls than boys went on the trip. How many girls went?
    Boys are compared to girls. We know the smaller part. To find the bigger part, add 95 and 42.

95 boys	42
? girls	

  o 122 girls went on the field trip. 42 fewer boys than girls went on the trip. How many boys went on the field trip?
    Girls are compared to boys. We know the bigger part. To find the smaller part, subtract 42 from 122.

122 girls	42
? boys	

  o There are 18 fruit candies. There are 3 times as many chocolate candies as fruit candies. How many chocolate candies are there?
    Two parts are compared. One is a multiple of the other. The smaller part is given. To find the smaller part, multiply 18 by 3 or add 18 three times.

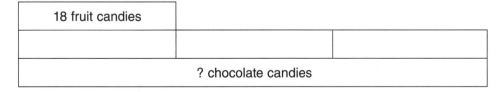

(Continued)

Table 5.14 (Continued)

Strategies

o A student buys 18 candies. 2/3 of the candies are fruit candies. How many fruit candies are there?

  The whole is given. To find 2/3 of the whole, multiply by 2/3 or divide 18 into thirds and add two of the thirds.

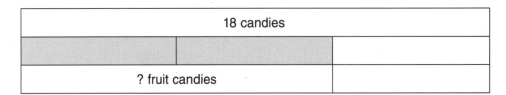

o David spent 2/5 of his money on a storybook. The storybook cost $20. How much money did he have at first?

  The part is given in both fraction and numeral form. To find the whole, divide by 2/5 or divide 20 in half and multiply by 5 (or add five times).

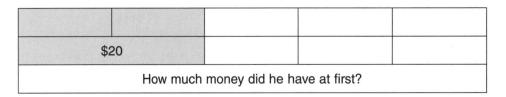

- *CUBS.* Teachers can and should develop operation word charts with their students as they engage in word problem solving. Students should solve word problems, first orally and then by reading questions, every day beginning in Kindergarten. Operation word charts can help students identify the operations that are represented by key terms. Teachers may also use a generic strategy such as CUBS to help students attack word problems. Using CUBS, students Circle numbers, in both numeral and word form; Underline operation words; Box what the question is asking them to find; and State the answer, leaving a space for the ultimate solution.

  For example, Ernesto sells newspapers. He sold ⌐114¬ papers on Monday. He sold ⌐78¬ papers on Tuesday. ⌐What is the total amount of newspapers Ernesto sold⌐? Ernesto sold a total of _____ newspapers, or The sum of newspapers that Ernesto sold was _____.

- *Guess and check.* Teachers should explicitly teach students to organize their guessing and checking, which provides a foundation for algebra. Start by making a reasonable guess at the solution to a problem, then apply all of the steps to the initial guess, and check if the answer is too high or low, adjusting subsequent guesses accordingly. Tables are used to organize guesses. For example, Sophie plays 115 iPod games. Ten are animal games; the rest are word and puzzle games. She plays twice as many word as puzzle games. How many puzzle games does she play?

  o Students identify key pieces of information, repeatedly reading the problem and paraphrasing the problem. For example, "I know there are twice as many word games as puzzle games. There are 10 animal games. The total number of games is 115." Students create a table to organize their guessing and checking.

Strategies				
Guess the Number of Puzzle Games	**The Number of Word Games (twice the number of puzzle games)**	**The Number of Animal Games (always 10)**	**Total (add the number of puzzle, word, and animal games)**	**Too High or Too Low?**
10	20	10	40	Too low
20	40	10	70	Too low
50	100	10	160	Too high
40	80	10	130	Too high
30	60	10	100	Too low
35	70	10	115	✓

- *Models and visual representations.* Teach students to use basic drawings, lines, or numbers to help visualize a mathematics problem. For example, 4 students were standing in line at lunch. Juliana was behind Summer. Itzel was between Juliana and Summer. Juliana was in front of Chloe. Who was the last student to receive lunch?

  o After reading the question to identify key information, students draw a picture that represents the problem, adding details as they reread.

  (front of line)—Summer—Juliana (back of line)

  (front of line)—Summer—Itzel—Juliana (back of line)

  (front of line)—Summer—Itzel—Juliana—Chloe (back of line)

Purchasing Mathematics Programs

In our experiences, targeted, intensive mathematics interventions are hard to find. There are, however, computer-based supports that we have found increase student learning in the very areas in which students typically most need support: computation, fractions, and word problems. These computer-based interventions, from Tom Snyder Productions and Scholastic, are

- FASTT Math,
- Fraction Nation, and
- GO Solve™ Word Problems.

There is also a web-based program that provides students with standards-specific practice, combined with a modicum of instruction and the option to record student performance, found at www.IXL.com.

Scaffolds and Accommodations to Access Core Content

Students who do not have number sense and/or cannot compute fluently with whole numbers, multidigit whole numbers, fractions, and decimals will experience difficulties in mathematics at nearly every grade level. To support all students, but particularly students for whom these number sense deficits exist, consider the following tools and strategies:

- Manipulatives, cubes (rod and flats), graph paper
- Hundreds chart
- Times table
- Graph paper
- Reduce the "size" and cognitive load of numbers:

    o Instead of $786 + 847$, assign $314 + 230$ or $78 + 84$.

    o Instead of $\dfrac{3}{4}x - \dfrac{1}{2} = \dfrac{5}{6}$, assign $4x - 5 = 13$

- Provide "cloze"-type supports, or partial solutions, of the algorithm or for the solution.
- For word problems, consider scaffolding by

    o reading the problems with students;
    o highlighting key words and phrases;
    o providing a visual support for the word problem;
    o providing the "Answer Frame" for the problem; and
    o reducing the magnitude of the numbers within the problem.

- We do not recommend that teachers remove the words from word problems; it is too important for students to tackle them.

Steps can also be critical and helpful for all students, but particularly students at risk, as temporary scaffolds. Steps are typically highly procedural in nature and their use should be complemented by conceptual reinforcement. Well-designed steps help teachers explain the how and why behind mathematical thinking; they represent a task analysis of the problem-solving process. Steps help students monitor their own problem solving early in their development of proficiency, so they can later apply these skills to new situations. Finally, steps can, when used in this iterative way, help teachers identify where student understanding is breaking down; in this way, they can serve as an error analysis tool as outlined in Table 5.15.

Table 5.15 Sample Steps

Rounding Numbers

1. Underline the word that comes after "nearest."

2. Underline the digit in the indicated place.

3. Circle the digit to the right of the underlined place.

4. If the circled digit is 5 or greater, add 1 to the underlined place and change all digits to the right to 0.

5. If the circled digit is 4 or less, keep the underlined place and change all digits to the right to 0.

Volume of a Solid

1. Write the volume formula.

2. Find the length, width, and height.

3. Multiply.

OR

1. Count the number of unit cubes.

Multiplying Multidigit Numbers by One-Digit Numbers

1. Rewrite in working form.

2. Multiply the ones place by the ones place (regroup if necessary).

3. Multiply the tens place by the ones place (add the regrouped digit and regroup again if necessary).

4. Continue with the hundreds place by the ones place, and so on.

Strategies for academic intervention are highly in demand and we believe that the resources above (Table 5.15), resources that we have used in our schools, will serve staff and students well. Schools are increasingly realizing, however, that academic interventions are not enough. Schools are even more hungry for strategies that help students improve their behavior. The next chapter will describe interventions that schools can utilize to address student needs in the areas of social and academic behaviors.

6

Social and Academic Behavioral Interventions

Behavioral competencies are at least as important as academic competencies to ensure that all students graduate from high school ready to pursue postsecondary opportunities. This chapter continues the work of Chapter 5—providing detailed, research-based interventions for students who have not yet responded to instruction and intervention. This chapter focuses on social and academic behavioral interventions.

SOCIAL BEHAVIORS

As noted in Chapter 1, a majority of schools with and in which we have worked would benefit from a more consistent positive schoolwide set of core behavioral norms and routines. This means that classrooms within grade levels and between grades have the same sets of expectations. Tier 1 is critical.

A well-defined and well-supported Tier 1 will lead to a more-successful Tier 2. Tier 2 behavioral supports should revolve around more-frequent and more-targeted strategies within the classroom, supported and defined by the administrators and clinicians at the school. At the beginning of this chapter, we stated that Tier 2 academic supports should provide more time and different types of supports for students to master prioritized content of the grade or course; Tier 2 behavioral supports should also relate to the Tier 1 behavioral expectations that have been established. We will detail a concise list of behavioral strategies in Table 6.1, but we want to ensure that our first line of defense is a well-established and supported Tier 1, followed by more-specialized strategies related to Tier 1 expectations, perhaps with more-frequent monitoring by staff and the student, that we will call Tier 2. When students do not respond to these levels of support, schools should provide more-intensive small group or individual supports outside the classroom, led and informed by specialists and clinicians, connected and related to the supports in classrooms. We will identify specific and intensive Tier 3 supports toward the end of the chapter in the "Tier 3 Behavioral Supports" section.

We believe that almost every incidence of student misbehavior is a symptom stemming from a separate but related antecedent cause. Identify the cause and provide support, and the misbehaviors will diminish and disappear. However, treating the symptom—that is, providing supports that are related to the misbehavior itself—or providing negative consequences in response to misbehavior, is unlikely to significantly or permanently change the behaviors. The interventions, or strategies, provided in Table 6.1 are research-based (Boynton & Boynton, 2005; Braithwaite, 2001; Brock, 1998; Carnine, 1976; DuPaul & Ervin, 1996; DuPaul & Stoner, 2003; Ford, Olmi, Edwards, & Tingstrom, 2001; Gettinger, 1988; Gettinger & Seibert, 2002; Heward, 1994; Lanceley, 1999; Long, Morse, & Newman, 1980; Martens & Kelly, 1993; Martens & Meller, 1990; Mayer, 2000 ; Mayer & Ybarra, 2004; Powell & Nelson, 1997; Sprick, Borgmeier, & Nolet, 2002; Thompson & Jenkins, 1993; U.S. Department of Education, 2004; Walker, 1997; Walker, Colvin, & Ramsey, 1995; Walker & Walker, 1991) and will help all students, but particularly students with asocial behaviors, to experience more success in class and school. Remember, strategies are only effective when they are

- preceded by teaching or reteaching of the desired skill or behavior;
- employed with a belief in the student and the strategy;
- used consistently, amongst staff, throughout the lesson, and day to day;
- combined with an effort to build a more-positive relationship with the student;
- reinforced with positive feedback;
- patiently and specifically corrected with feedback; and
- monitored with data, by both student and staff.

Implicit in the social behavior strategies—the Tier 2 behavioral interventions—is that the school, and every staff member within the school, has been providing and is providing core, Tier 1 instruction in these critical areas (Table 6.1).

Table 6.1   Social Behavior Strategies

Goal Area	Strategy
Cooperation (disruption)	• Teach students to gather data on their own behavior and guide them to reflect on the frequencies and reasons behind the numbers. • Use precorrection cards, such as those provided in Table 6.2, to remind students to perform their best when they are most vulnerable. These crucial moments can be discovered using the behavioral diagnostics described in Chapter 4. • Provide two minutes of time with a teacher or peer when the student has successfully delayed his or her need for attention—that is, when the student has made the decision not to disrupt. • Create a crate of activities, academic and less-academic, with which the students can interact and play for a defined period of time when they feel the need, instead of disrupting learning. • Teach conflict resolution skills to the student (or all students in the class), when disruptions are due to student-to-student disagreements. • Provide a second description of directions and expectations to students who have proven to need such attention to avoid future, but likely predictable, disruptions from occurring when a student should be working more independently. • Give brief, gentle signals to students just beginning to misbehave—either with a quiet word to the student (verbal), with a significant look (nonverbal), or through a precorrection card. If it's predictable, it's preventable. • Help label the emotion in an effort to de-escalate situations by acknowledging feelings when a student seems upset, helping students directly state the emotion rather than communicating it indirectly through behaviors. Once an emotion is labeled, staff and student can identify triggers and find solutions. • Award the student a certain number of behavior points at the start of a period or lesson and/or write that number of tally marks on the board to improve feedback and monitoring (by both staff and the student). Privately inform the student that each time the student disrupts learning, a staff member will silently remove one point from the student's total. The student keeps any remaining behavior points; points earned over multiple days can be redeemed for prizes or privileges. • Give students praise and attention only when they are on task; disruptive students will be likely to attend more frequently. Make an effort to identify those (initially) infrequent times when the student is appropriately focused; immediately give positive attention through verbal praise, encouragement, and friendly eye contact. • Redirect overactive students using a silent signal. Meet with the student to identify disruptive behaviors, then select a silent signal to be used to alert the student that behavior has crossed a threshold and now is distracting. Role-play and practice scenarios and positively reinforce decisions to respond appropriately to signals. • Meet privately to discuss which behaviors are distracting. What is monitored receives our attention most. Students often change problem behaviors when

Table 6.1 (Continued)

Goal Area	Strategy
Cooperation (disruption) (*continued*)	they pay attention to those behaviors. Together with the student, design a simple distractible-behavior rating form. Have the student rate his or her behaviors at the end of each class period. Positively reinforce the student for accuracy and improvement.
	• Chunk tasks into small parts and have students submit their work to a staff member or another student before proceeding to the next small part when the student's disruptions are caused by rushing through an assignment or by straying from the completion of a task.
	• Avoid using negative phrasing whenever possible, (e.g., "If you don't return to your seat, I can't help you with your assignment"). When a request has a positive spin, a power struggle is less likely and students are more likely to comply. Instead, restate requests in positive terms (e.g., "I will be over to help you on the assignment just as soon as you return to your seat").
	• When a disruption has occurred, assign a written or graphic report, with or without stems and frames, that addresses these questions:
	o "What did you do?" o "Why was that a bad thing to do?" o "What happened after you were disruptive?" o "How do you think your actions made people feel?" o "What were you trying to accomplish?" o "Next time you have that goal, how will you meet it without hurting anybody?"
Social respect (defiance)	• Praise, but use caution when praising defiant students. Do not embarrass. Ensure praise is sincere, specific, and not embarrassing. Deliver praise as soon as possible. For older students, consider writing a note, praising privately or with a look, or calling parents.
	• Keep responses calm, brief, and businesslike. Sarcasm and lengthy negative reprimands can trigger defiant student behavior. Instead, respond in a neutral, business-like, calm voice. Brief responses prevent staff from inadvertently rewarding misbehaving students with attention.
	• Listen actively. Project a sincere desire to understand and summarize student concerns. Model effective negotiation skills. Paraphrase, demonstrating respect for students' points of view. This can also enhance a student's understanding of the problem. Teachers are modeling a positive, effective behavior.
	• Help avoid a full-blown conflict by allowing the student to save face; students sometimes blunder into potential confrontations. Ask, "Is there anything that we can work out together so you can stay in the classroom and be successful?" Treat the student with dignity, model negotiation and conflict resolution skills, and demonstrate that adults respect and value students. Provide the student with a final chance to resolve the conflict and avoid more-serious consequences. Students may initially give a sarcastic or unrealistic response (e.g., "Yeah, you can leave me alone and stop trying to get me to do classwork!"). Ignore such power struggles and simply ask again whether there is a reasonable way to engage the student's cooperation.

Goal Area	Strategy
Social respect (defiance) *(continued)*	• Proactively intervene. Staff may interrupt escalating behaviors by redirecting student attention. If defiant behavior is just beginning, engage the student in a high-interest activity, such as playing an educational computer game or helping in the classroom. Or remove the student from the room to prevent escalation; send the student on an errand to provide him or her time to calm down. • Project calmness. Staff must control their own behavior when attempting to defuse a confrontation with a defiant student. Approach the student at a slow, deliberate pace and maintain a reasonable distance. Speak privately to the student in a calm and respectful voice. Avoid staring, hands on hips, or finger pointing. Keep comments brief. If negative behaviors escalate, move away from the student. • Give positive choices. When a student's disrespect indicates a need for control, structure requests to acknowledge the freedom to choose whether to comply or receive a logical consequence. Frame requests as a two-part statement. First, present the negative choice and its consequences, then state the positive behavioral choice that staff would like the student to select. • Assign a student at risk a responsibility-inducing job, such as serving as a scout. Scouts recognize students, at the end of a mini-lesson or time period, who have met classroom expectations, providing specific details about recognized students' appropriate behaviors. • Identify a corner of the room (or area outside the classroom with adult supervision) where students can take a brief break. Make breaks available to all students. When a student becomes upset and defiant, offer to talk the situation over once he or she has calmed down and then direct the student to the cool-down corner. • Ask neutral, open-ended questions to collect more information before responding when faced with a confrontational student. Pose *who, what, where, when,* and *how* questions to more fully understand the problem situation and identify possible solutions. Avoid asking *why* questions because they can imply that you are blaming the student, which may invite excuses. • Avoid arguments or unnecessary discussions when disciplining. Instead, move away from the student, repeat requests in a businesslike tone of voice, and impose a predetermined consequence for noncompliance.

Physical respect (aggression)	• Teach, reteach, and/or role-play strategies for identifying and respecting boundaries.
	 • Teach cognitive restructuring:
	   ○ The student describes the situation that resulted in the conflict or incident, and describes physical or emotional sensations.
	   ○ The student next describes her or his perspective on *why* the situation occurred, and also shares others' perspectives.
	   ○ The staff member challenges, extends, and corrects irrational perspectives, perhaps in a humorous, but respectful (not sarcastic) way.
	   ○ The student and the staff member construct a more-rational perspective that explains the causes of the situation.

(Continued)

Table 6.1 (Continued)

Goal Area	Strategy
Physical respect (aggression) *(continued)*	o The new explanation is applied and a new response is practiced. o The student agrees to record when the new response is used. o The staff member checks in with the student regularly to reinforce, remind, and reteach. • Guide students in using a 5-point emotional scale—A pictorial and/or numerical guide helps student label emotions and includes student/staff identified ways of coping. • Teach Stop-Walk-Talk o Students *Stop.* When students experience aggression or bullying, or witness aggression or bullying, they raise their hands to a "stop signal" and say, "Stop." *Walk.* When students have tried "stop" and the aggression or bullying continues, they walk away from the aggression or bullying, or if the student is the witness, walk away with the student experiencing the aggression or bullying. *Talk.* When the students have walked away, they talk to an adult. o Adults: Ask students to describe aggression or bullying. Ask students if they said, "Stop." Ask students if they walked away calmly. Follow up with all students. When students are asked to "stop," they immediately stop what they are doing, take a deep breath and count to 3, go on with the day, and talk to an adult as soon as possible to review the situation, their actions, and their reactions to "Stop." • Assign a written or graphic report, with or without stems and frames, that addresses these questions: o "What did you do?" o "Why was that a bad thing to do?" o "What happened after you were disruptive?" o "What were you trying to accomplish?" o "How do you think your actions made people feel?" o "Next time you have that goal, how will you meet it without hurting anybody?"

Goal Area	Strategy

Physical respect (aggression) *(continued)*	• Teach and practice a few of the following relaxation techniques to help students calm themselves:
	
	  ○ Deep breathing
	  ○ Count to 10
	  ○ Write in a journal
	  ○ Draw
	  ○ Color
	  ○ Scribble
	  ○ Read
	  ○ Visualize
	  ○ Listen to music or nature sounds
	  ○ Take a break

Verbal respect (inappropriate language)	• Provide, teach, and practice how to use replacement language "guides" that provide appropriate language as a replacement for inappropriate language. • Provide, teach, and practice how to use guides that provide appropriate language as a replacement for pictured emotions. • Design a simple inappropriate-language rating form. Have the student rate his or her behaviors at the end of each class period. Positively reinforce the student for accuracy and improvement. • Teach, reteach, and/or role-play strategies for using appropriate language in specific situations. • Students state or write, using appropriate language, a message to the individual(s) to whom the inappropriate language was directed as a form of restitution.
Attention (inattention)	• Provide students with a visible, tangible schedule of the lesson's, or day's, activities. When student styles are matched to pedagogy, improved on-task behavior is likely; improved behaviors also correlate with a brisk pace. Ensure that instruction is structured and brisk. To achieve a brisk pace, ensure full lesson preparation and minimize the time spent on housekeeping items and transitions. • Remove all items not needed for tasks. Distractible students behave better when their work area is uncluttered. • Select a peer who has a good relationship with the student and is not easily drawn off-task, and seek permission (from the student and parents) to appoint that student as a helper. Meet privately with the student and the helper. Tell the helper that whenever the student's verbal or motor behavior becomes distracting, the helper should give the student a brief, quiet, nonjudgmental signal (e.g., a light tap on the shoulder, a precorrection card). Role-play scenarios so the helper knows when to ignore and when to intervene. • Schedule tasks and time wisely. Save easier subjects or tasks for later in the lesson or day, when attention wanes. Avoid long stretches of instructional time in which students sit passively.

(Continued)

Table 6.1 (Continued)

Goal Area	Strategy
Attention (inattention) *(continued)*	• Capture students' attention. Employ predictable structures, routines, and procedures. Reinforce auditory directions with pictures and other visual supports. Give clear directions at a pace that does not overwhelm students. Post directions for later review. Give directions as a handout. Gain students' attention before giving directions. Use creative strategies (mnemonics, think-pair-share) to ensure full understanding. Call target students by name and establish eye contact before providing the directions. Use alerting cues such as, "One, two, three, eyes on me" to gain attention. Wait until all students are attending before giving directions. Give directions at a pace that does not overwhelm. State multistep directions one at a time and confirm that students are able to comply with each step before giving the next direction. Proactively and privately approach target students to reiterate and restate directions. Ask target students to repeat directions. • Keep students guessing. Randomly call on students, occasionally selecting the same student twice in a row or within a short time span. Pose a question to the class, give students wait time to formulate an answer (and/or use Think-Pair-Share), and then randomly call on a student. • Provide attention breaks. Contract with students to give them short breaks to engage in a preferred activity each time that target students have finished a given amount of work. Attention breaks can refresh the student—and also make the learning task more reinforcing. Modify contracts as behavior improves.
Self-control (impulsivity)	• Provide a quiet work area. A desk or study carrel in the corner of the room can serve as an appropriate workspace. When introducing these workspaces, stress that the quiet locations are intended to help students concentrate. Never use the area as a punishment. • Avoid long stretches of instructional time in which students sit passively. When students are actively engaged in an activity, they are more likely to be on task. Schedule instructional activities so that students must frequently show what they know through some kind of active response (e.g., think-pair-share with random selection, white boards) • Employ proximity control and assign preferential seating. Seat students where they are most likely to stay focused. Teachers focus instruction on a portion of the room; place the target student's seat somewhere within that zone. During whole-group activities, circulate the room. Stand or sit near the target student before giving directions or engaging in discussion. • Provide frequent motor breaks. The behaviors of active students improve when they are permitted to quietly walk around the classroom when they feel fidgety. Alternatively, allow students a discretionary pass to get a drink of water or walk up and down the hall. • Create motor outlets. When impulsivity involves playing with objects, substitute an alternative motor behavior that will not distract. Use stress balls, exercise bands wrapped around the legs of chairs, or other creative, nondisruptive outlets that meet the need for movement or physical feedback. • Transition quickly. Train students to transition appropriately by demonstrating how they should prepare for common academic activities, such as whole

Goal Area	Strategy
Self-control (impulsivity) *(continued)*	group, small group, and independent work. Practice these transitions, praising the group for timely and correct performance. Provide additional coaching to target students as needed. Verbally alert students several minutes before a transition. • Cocreate advance organizers. Give students a quick overview of the activities planned for the instructional period or day, providing students with a visual and/or mental schedule, how activities interrelate, the important materials that will be needed, and the amount of time for each activity.

Attendance (absences)	• Conduct a simplified FBA focused on "why" the student is absent, considering
	
	   o health (involve nurse);
	   o emotional needs (involve counselors or social workers);
	   o academic needs (review student performance, involve teachers); and
	   o potential bullying (involve peers).
	
	• Develop a plan to address the antecedents to absences (the "why" behind absences); share plan with all stakeholders; establish goals.
	• Identify temporary positive reinforcers when goals are met.

Honesty (lying/ cheating/ stealing)	• Conduct a simplified FBA focused on "why" the student is lying, cheating, or stealing, considering the following:
	
	   o *Need.* Does the student have basic personal needs?
	   o *Academic deficits.* Is there an academic need that contributes to dishonesty?
	   o *Physical or emotional anxiety.* Does the student fear repercussions, rationally or irrationally?
	
	• *Student written report.* Assign a written or graphic report, with or without stems and frames, that addresses these questions:
	
	   o "What did you say or do?"
	   o "Why was that a dishonest thing to say or do?"
	   o "What did you mean to say or do?"
	   o "How do you think your words or actions made people feel?"
	   o "What were you trying to accomplish?"
	   o "Next time you have that goal, how will you meet that need without hurting anybody?"

Empathy (harassment/ bullying)	• Explicitly teach empathy (the ability to understand and experience the feelings of others, and to respond in helpful ways):
	
	   o *Model.* The best way to teach empathy is to model empathy. Staff publicly support students when they experience a difficulty, label feelings and acknowledge that they've felt that way, and listen actively. Attempt to talk a student through a challenge and respond to difficult situations thoughtfully.
	   o *Meet emotional needs.* Kids are more likely to develop empathy when their emotional needs are met. Strive to ensure that students are heard and helped when things are hard. Provide security; build relationships between adults and students and students and students.

(Continued)

Table 6.1 (Continued)

Goal Area	Strategy
Empathy (harassment/ bullying) (continued)	o *Teach feelings identification.* Label positive and negative feelings so students can connect feelings with reactions, as well as identify those feelings in others. Understanding a person or behavior depends on understanding feelings. o *Use games.* Have students make "feelings" faces in the mirror with peers, and guess what each face represents. Share experiences with these feelings. Explain that you can experience emotions by just imagining them. Or, take turns acting out and guessing feelings. Or, guess feelings during shared reading, identifying words and nonverbal cues from pictures, and brainstorming ways to empathize with characters. o *Teach and assign responsibilities.* Classroom responsibilities enhance empathy and caring, particularly when they involve responsibility to or for others. o *Teach problem-solving skills.* Provide students with the opportunity and responsibility to solve their own problems, perhaps using Stop-Think-Act. *Stop.* Assess the situation and determine the problem. *Think.* Consider possible solutions. *Act.* Choose the best option and put it into action. • Practice "I'm with you" statements, communicating empathy, acceptance, and understanding using students' own experiences: o "I might make that same mistake." o "Lots of us feel that way." o "I can see how you would do that." o "I understand why you would say that." • Assign older children to mentor younger children, even when one or both students have displayed behavioral challenges. Ensure all staff involved is willing and prepared. "Train" students to perform as mentors. Young students refer to older mentors as "Mr. John" or "Ms. Susie." Observe, debrief, and analyze with the mentor. • Teach, model, and practice relationship building. o Teach lessons on relationships, friendships, getting along with others, and tolerance o Model and role-play relationship skills, such as involving others, particularly students who are not often chosen, sharing resources, and assisting others. o Explicitly teach, model, practice, and reinforce collaborative group work.

ACADEMIC BEHAVIORS

When students do not possess an adequate knowledge of the rules of school, and/or when they do not put into practice the organizational and study skills that support academic success, we must provide explicit instruction and/or interventions in these areas. Sometimes known as self-regulatory strategies or executive functioning skills, the academic behaviors that we defined in

Table 6.2 Precorrection Card Samples

You can do it!! Remember to keep your hands, feet, and objects to yourself. ☺ ☺ ☺ ☺ ☺ ☺ ☺ ☺ ☺ ☺	You can do it!! Remember to keep your eyes on the teacher and sit like a scholar. ☺ ☺ ☺ ☺ ☺ ☺ ☺ ☺ ☺ ☺
You can do it!! Remember to stay on task. ☺ ☺ ☺ ☺ ☺ ☺ ☺ ☺ ☺ ☺	You can do it!! Remember to follow directions right away. ☺ ☺ ☺ ☺ ☺ ☺ ☺ ☺ ☺ ☺
You can do it!! Remember to help your partners. ☺ ☺ ☺ ☺ ☺ ☺ ☺ ☺ ☺ ☺	You can do it!! Remember to take a breath and use your words when frustrated. ☺ ☺ ☺ ☺ ☺ ☺ ☺ ☺ ☺ ☺
You can do it!! Remember to use kind words. ☺ ☺ ☺ ☺ ☺ ☺ ☺ ☺ ☺ ☺	Nice work!! Your behavior toward your classmates is great today! ☺ ☺ ☺ ☺ ☺ ☺ ☺ ☺ ☺ ☺
You can do it!! Remember to do kind things for your classmates. ☺ ☺ ☺ ☺ ☺ ☺ ☺ ☺ ☺ ☺	Nice work!! I love the way you're working today! ☺ ☺ ☺ ☺ ☺ ☺ ☺ ☺ ☺ ☺

Chapter 2 are critical to success in school and in life. When students demonstrate a lack of success in these areas, we must provide more instruction and/or intervention. Consider the approaches in Tables 6.3 and 6.4. As with all interventions, the idea is not that these supports are provided indefinitely; we want to transition to a less-restrictive environment. Instead, research suggests that students must have one hundred useful repetitions (successes or failures for which a constructive reflection has occurred) to change habits (Benson, 2012).

Table 6.3 Academic Behavior Strategies

Goal Area	Strategy
Metacognitive practices (rote learning)	• Teach students to connect new lessons and subjects to life and other subjects in school. • Teach students to pause every few minutes to think about learning. • Ensure that lessons and units begin and end with concrete, collaborative discussions about, "What are we learning?" "Why are we learning it?" Provide time throughout lessons for these reflections. • Model metacognition at all times, in "think-alouds" related to academic and behavioral learning.

Growth mindset and positive self-concept (fixed mindset and negative self-talk)	• Identify, describe, revisit, and build off strengths.
	• Use praise and corrections carefully. Avoid
	
	   ○ "No _____-ing!"
	   ○ "Good job!"
	   ○ "Don't argue with me."
	   ○ "Wait until _____ finds out about this."
	   ○ "If you do that one more time . . . ."
	   ○ "You are doing that the wrong way."
	   ○ "That is what happens when you . . . ."
	   ○ "You can't do that."
	   ○ "Don't do that."
	   ○ "We are _____-ing right now, OKAY?"
	   ○ "You are making me really mad right now."
	
	• Do not use sarcasm.
	• Recognize students for improvement and acknowledge the effort needed to learn . . . always!
	• Engage students in journaling and reflective dialogue: "Imagine yourself ten years from now. What would your wiser self say about this situation?"
	• Teach students to set long-term goals and make short-term plans to reach them.
	• Teach students to identify positive attributes of various phenomena in themselves and in others (from body parts to written assignments). Model these practices.
	• Teach students to assess their own work using a simple rubric and to plot their performance, so that they can view their progress over time.

Goal Area	Strategy

Growth mind and positive self-concept (fixed mindset and negative self-talk) *(continued)*	• Teach students to be aware of attitudes about school and motivation for learning. "Whether you think you can or think you can't, you're right." Model and reinforce the veracity of Henry Ford's phrase.
	• Teach students to talk to an adult when worried about school. Teach students techniques for coping with worry.
	• Build in rewarding opportunities for social interaction. A student may find an otherwise tedious or frustrating task to be more motivating if it provides an opportunity for social interaction. An adult tutor can provide support and encouragement that can kindle motivation for a student. Cross-age peer tutoring, cooperative learning groups, and study groups are other examples of social situations that students may find to be both motivating and good settings for reviewing academic skills.
	• Validate, normalize, identify, and instill
	
	    ○ Validate what a student is experiencing: "I know you are frustrated because you think that this assignment is too hard."
	    ○ Normalize the feeling: "I get frustrated when I think something is hard and so do other students."
	    ○ Identify a time when the student was able to complete a difficult assignment: "Remember when we did that math sheet and you felt you couldn't do it and you got all of them right?"
	    ○ Instill confidence in the student: "I know you can do it and I think you know you can too."
	
	• Equip students to act as peer tutors
	
	    ○ You can be subtle and suggest frequently that a certain student (who you know is confident) work with, play with, help, eat lunch with, or assist, a student who is less confident, isolated, withdrawn, or shy.
	    ○ You may be more formal with the intervention and speak with a confident student, asking him or her to interact more and help another specific student to "come out of (her or his) shell," participate more, and be more confident and outgoing. You may or may not choose to explain this to the less-confident student.
	    ○ You may speak with the less-confident, withdrawn, or shy student explaining that you would like him or her to try to work more often with another specific student (who you know is confident).
	    ○ When choosing partners for assignments or choosing groups for projects, make a point to place less-confident students with more-confident students.
	    ○ Praise students frequently when they exhibit confidence.
	    ○ You may consider giving rewards or a note home for students who exhibit certain behaviors that portray confidence, like sharing something with the class or volunteering a certain number of times.
	
	• Post the affirmations in Table 6.4 and provide students with frequent opportunities to practice self-talk that involves these positive statements.

Table 6.3 (Continued)

Goal Area	Strategy
Self-monitoring/ Internal locus of control (external loci of control)	• Teach students about self-assessing to ensure learning has occurred. • Teach students specific ways to review new content. • Teach students how to monitor understanding when reading and learning. • Teach students how to prepare for classes. • Create and reflect on "visual steps" with students: "I just did . . . now I'm doing . . . next . . . "
Engagement/ motivation (apathy)	• Take responsibility for motivating students. Whether we like it or not, students are constantly expecting and collecting feedback from their teachers. Teachers need to be aware of the impact that verbal comments and nonverbal body language have on their students' motivation level. • Teach students to set short-term goals for individual tasks and assignments. • Transform tasks into mini-contests. • Coconstruct "futures" with students and teach students to place themselves in that future—reference this practice through lessons and units. • Coconstruct goals with students, and connect tasks—small and large—to these goals. • Engineer early victories. Ensure students taste success, and systematically build off these successes. • Explicitly teach techniques for self-discipline. • Assign a classroom job (e.g., scout, materials organizer). • Make activities stimulating. Choose contexts that you think will appeal to students (e.g., sports, fashion). Help students to see a valuable real-word pay-off for learning the material being taught. Students who don't learn well in traditional lecture format may show higher rates of engagement when interacting with peers or when allowed the autonomy and self-pacing of computer-delivered instruction. • Provide audiences for student work. Specify an audience for whom students are preparing their creative work. Encourage students to submit their work to publications, post it on websites, or present it to audiences. • Connect academic requirements to real-world situations. When students see that content covered in their coursework can help to explain how actual, high-profile problems were created or solved, they can sense the real power of academic knowledge and its potential to affect human lives. Tasks should be meaningful and relevant to the learner. The aim of tasks should be to improve or gain some skill rather than rote memorization of irrelevant facts. • Give opportunities for choice. Allowing students a choice in their instructional activities boosts attention span and increases engagement. Make a list of choice options that you are comfortable offering students during typical learning activities. Give students as much control over their own education as possible. Let students choose paper and project topics that interest them. Assess students in a variety of ways (e.g., tests, papers, projects, presentations). Give students options for how these assignments are weighted. Provide students with a say in what the task is, as well as how it is to be carried out and presented. Allow students to select the order

Goal Area	Strategy
Engagement/ motivation (apathy) *(continued)*	in which they will complete several in-class or homework assignments. Allow students to take short, timed breaks during a work period and allow them to choose when to take them. • Make learning fun. Use game-like formats to liven up academic material and engage student interest. • Minimize pressures on students. Remove competition or social comparisons; revise grading systems. • Appropriately acknowledge students for performance and growth. Use praise liberally. Reward for effort and improvement and not just for performance. • Structure learning. Ensure instructions are clear. Students must know the learning target—what they must know and be able to do. Guidelines on how the task is to be performed must be specific and well understood. Immediate and useful feedback is crucial. A promptly returned assignment with comments indicating where the student went wrong and how he or she could improve is much more useful than a paper with only a B or C grade on it. • Foster a supportive environment. Students do not perform or think well when they feel invalidated or threatened. The rapport that teachers develop with the student must be one of ease and comfort—an encouraging word or tone of voice, a hand on the shoulder. • Show honest appreciation. Use "I statements" to convey honest appreciation about a student, communicating personal appreciation, rather than using a mechanical or an exaggerated response: "I appreciate that." "I like the way you said that." "Thank you very much for that." "I sure like that you took that risk." • Provide attention without praise. Simply give time and attention to a student by listening carefully, supporting and encouraging without causing the student to grow dependent on teacher approval or praise. Use honest appreciation or "I'm with you." Use nonthreatening physical touch like a pat on the arm or shaking hands. Use sincere eye contact that shows you are truly listening. Give students time so you can listen or communicate with them about a situation. Greet students after their absences. Respond that an answer was simply correct or incorrect, treating the students like intelligent people who do not appreciate overstatements or exaggerations: "Yes, that's right." "Okay." "Yes, that's just what I wanted." "Correct." "Yes, thank you." "You had the first part right, but the last part was incorrect." "Thank you for taking a risk to answer." • Provide praise and acknowledgement for all. Be free with praise and constructive in criticism. Negative comments should pertain to particular performances, not the performer. Offer nonjudgmental feedback on students' work, stress opportunities to improve, look for ways to stimulate advancement, and avoid dividing students into sheep and goats. Be fair in distributing praise; all students should receive praise. Look for positive things to say about a student's work even when pointing out problems or mistakes with the work. Praise the entire class to encourage and build unity. Focus on the use of praise to motivate continuous improvement.

Table 6.3 (Continued)

Goal Area	Strategy
Engagement/ motivation (apathy) *(continued)*	• Promote fairness and avoid exaggeration. Consciously react positively to all students; put personal differences aside and treat each student equally so each student has the same opportunity to be motivated to learn. Be wary of the manipulation that may happen when we focus attention on the positive behavior of a student or group in order to hint that another behavior is the most desirable. While this works in some situations to motivate students to modify their behavior, it may be interpreted as manipulation. Consider avoiding, "Look at how well Sally did on the assignment." "I really like how well this side of the room is contributing." Exaggeration can devalue honest relationships between students and teachers. Exaggerated praise includes, "Great answer!" "Super!" "Wonderful!" "Sensational!" Be specific with praise. When these kinds of statements are used repetitively, students are not encouraged to be intrinsically motivated. • Develop self-motivated learners. Encourage lifelong learning and learning for the sake of learning. Become a role model for student interest. Deliver your presentations with energy and enthusiasm. Teacher passion motivates students. Make the course personal, showing why you are interested in the material. • Get to know students. Knowledge of student concerns and backgrounds, and personal interest in them, inspire loyalty to the teacher, to the course, and to learning. Display a strong interest in students' learning and a faith in their abilities. • Use examples freely. Students want to be shown why a concept or technique is useful before they want to study it further. • Teach by discovery. Whenever possible, allow students to reason through a problem and discover the underlying principles. Cooperative learning activities are particularly effective because they also provide positive social pressure. Allow students to struggle for a reasonable amount of time before providing the answer. • Set realistic performance goals, then help students achieve them. Encourage students to set their own reasonable goals. Design assignments that are appropriately challenging in view of the experience and aptitude of the class. • Place appropriate emphasis on testing and grading. Tests should be a means of showing what students have mastered, not what they have not. Avoid grading on the curve and give everyone the opportunity to achieve the highest standard and grades. • Involve parents. Share all techniques with parents. Encourage them to reinforce motivational techniques used at school.
Strategy creation and use (passive learning)	• Adopt a schoolwide way of organizing learning, from binders to notes. • Teach students ways to organize new learning: o Acronyms/mnemonics o Memorization techniques o Restating/rewriting notes

Goal Area	Strategy

Strategy creation and use (passive learning) *(continued)*	• Explicitly teach students study aids:
	
	  o How to identify the most important information
	  o About to use study aides provided in textbooks
	  o How to create their own study aides
	  o How to prepare for tests and how to create a plan of attack for taking a test
	  o About different types of tests and test questions
	  o How to reason through to an answer
	
	• Model these strategies, provide students with practice using these strategies, and give feedback on their employment.

Volition and perseverance (giving up)	• Explicitly teach students how to create and follow a schedule:
	
	  o How to deal with distractions, competing goals, and procrastination
	  o How to better concentrate
	  o To prioritize
	  o To establish and work toward external or internal incentives
	  o To visualize and reference the habits of heroes
	
	• For students requiring supplemental support with volition, reduce length of assignments. Chunk assignments, even assigning only one task at a time. For new material, trim assignments to the minimum length that you judge will ensure student understanding. When having students practice skills or review previously taught material, break that review into a series of short assignments rather than one long assignment to help sustain interest and engagement.
	• Differentiate the types of tasks assigned to students. Ensure that tasks are within each student's zone of proximal development.
	• Explicitly teach, consistently reference, and ensure that students follow the School and Student Affirmations for Students in Table 6.4.

Resiliency (emotional crises)	• Explicitly teach and model coping skills.
	• Guide students in using a visual or written "rating the intensity of emotions" guide to label and appropriately manage their feelings.
	• Teach, model, and practice self-talk scripts.
	
	  o The staff member and the student create a script that defines thoughts, words, and actions that the student can follow in target situations.
	  o The staff member first practices use of the script with the student; the script can be followed verbatim by the student during the first few uses.
	  o Use of the explicit script is faded as behaviors improve.
	  o The staff member checks in with the student regularly to reinforce, remind, and reteach.
	
	• Assign journaling and promote the practice as a healthy reflective tool.
	• Ensure that students know how to access adults, and which adults to access.

Table 6.3 (Continued)

Goal Area	Strategy

Resiliency (emotional crises) (continued)	• Prepare an "emotional plan" with students. Role-play different situations and how students should emotionally respond.
	• Provide the opportunities to use nondisruptive, tactile stress relief.
	• Encourage students to reward themselves for dealing with difficult situations well.
	• Teach relaxation techniques:
	   ○ Deep breathing
	   ○ Count to 10
	   ○ Write in a journal
	   ○ Draw
	   ○ Color
	   ○ Scribble
	   ○ Read
	   ○ Visualization
	   ○ Listen to music or nature sounds
	   ○ Take a break

Table 6.4 School and Student Affirmations for Students

- I can do whatever I focus my mind on.
- I am awesome.
- I am intelligent.
- I am a fast learner.
- I am worthy.
- I love and accept myself.
- I enjoy learning.
- Learning is fun and exciting.
- I understand the lessons taught in school completely.
- I believe in myself and in my abilities.
- While I appreciate details, I am also able to see the big picture.
- I have many gifts and talents.
- I learn from my challenges and can always find ways to overcome them.
- I am open to possibilities.
- I embrace my fears fully and calmly.
- I make like-minded friends easily and naturally.
- I am healthy and am growing up well.
- I am persistent.
- I am creative.
- I have ideas for solving problems.
- I am a great listener.
- I am kind, generous, and loving.
- I complete my school work on time every day.
- I achieve great and successful results.
- I am brave.
- I have an awesome imagination.
- I am able to solve problems creatively.
- I am thankful.
- I have a healthy relationship with my teachers.
- I choose to forgive others.
- I feel confident and secure.
- I enjoy letting events unfold in good time.
- I have loving, positive, and happy thoughts.
- I enjoy expressing my ideas.
- I am courageous even when things are unknown to me.
- I reach my goals.
- I am in charge of my own life.
- I enjoy playing games with my friends.
- I have many friends who like being near me.
- I am becoming good at math, reading, writing.
- I absorb knowledge like a sponge and am able to apply what I have learned.

- My family, friends, and teachers love me.
- I am unique and special.
- I may make mistakes sometimes, but I choose to learn from them.
- I accept myself even though I sometimes make mistakes.
- Every day and in every way, I get better and better.
- I am calm, relaxed, and peaceful.
- I am always in the right place at the right time.
- I enjoy being, feeling, and thinking positive.
- Problems challenge me to be better.
- I trust myself to make great decisions.
- I am kind to everyone.
- I do my best in my work and tasks.
- I enjoy my own company.
- I accept compliments graciously and openly.
- I am whole and complete.
- I enjoy trying new ideas.
- I embrace changes in peaceful, harmonious, and positive ways.
- I believe I can be whatever I want to be.
- I can visualize well.
- I am vibrant and have lots of energy.

- I do my best for my studies.
- I am attentive in class.
- I am a natural.
- I am on top of my classes.
- I enjoy challenging myself with new ideas, possibilities, and directions.
- I am a winner!
- I turn failures into opportunities for success.
- I handle all my responsibilities and tasks well.
- I enjoy healthy snacks.
- I love my body.
- I am honest and trustworthy.
- I choose to look for the best way forward for myself.
- I am able to understand and solve complex problem or questions.
- I love being healthy!
- I manage my time well.
- I like being punctual.
- I enjoy having habits that will help me have a happy, healthy, and successful life.
- I draw inspiration from nature and life.
- I believe in my dreams.
- I have an excellent memory.

All students, but particularly those for whom motivation and organization are inhibiting their success, will benefit from explicit instruction and intervention with academic behaviors. Consider explicitly teaching the following study skills, or Steps to Academic Success, to students with poor work habits and work completion (see Table 6.5).

Given the limited time available within the school day to intervene with students in multiple domains, and the fact that academic and behavioral needs are interrelated, we advocate blending the practice and reinforcement of certain behaviors within academic, small-group interventions. For the unit (one week, two weeks, one month) during which the intervention groups meets, the interventionist would introduce a behavior strategy to the students at the beginning of the week. The interventionists would then repeatedly model, while the students would repeatedly practice, the skills, with the interventionist providing corrective feedback and positive reinforcement. Integrating behavioral support within an academic intervention is efficient and also provides a meaningful context within which behaviors can be practiced. While several minutes of each academic intervention will be spent providing support for the target behavior, we believe that the trade-off is worthwhile. Consider the scope and sequence that lists behavioral skills that could be introduced, modeled, practiced, and reinforced during different weeks of an academic intervention (see Table 6.6).

Table 6.5   Steps to Academic Success

1. Setting goals and establishing a due date
2. Planning, prioritizing, and sequencing the steps or tasks needed to reach the goal
3. Identifying necessary information and/or materials
4. Obtaining and organizing the information and/or materials needed to complete the goal
5. Beginning the task
6. Persevering through distractions and delaying gratification
7. Establishing a reasonable work rate so that the goal is met by the due date
8. Shifting form one task to another smoothly
9. Responding to, and incorporating, feedback
10. Assessing performance and progress toward the goal
11. Controlling emotional responses to difficult situations
12. Seeing tasks through to completion

Negative Consequences

While we have not heretofore devoted space to negative consequences, or provided recommendations on creative ways to punish students, we acknowledge that such consequences are appropriate at times. We ask that when administering negative consequences teachers

- commit to problem-solving with colleagues to identify the causes, antecedents, and/or functions of misbehavior;
- consider how adult behaviors or environmental factors may be exacerbating the misbehavior;
- commit to teaching or reteaching the desired behavior to the offending student; and
- commit to positively reinforcing the student when those desired behaviors are displayed.

Here are more thoughts on negative consequences:

We tend to use the word *punishment* to describe negative consequences imposed on students when they misbehave. The word has moral overtones, suggesting that students being punished deserve the punishment because their actions violate a rule, law, or expectation. In the field of behavior management, punishment (or negative consequences) has a more narrow and neutral definition: the presentation or removal of events that leads to a reduction in a target behavior (Kazdin, 1989). Events that serve to decrease an individual's behaviors are considered to be punishers. Teachers should understand the pros and cons of using punishment; schools nearly always build punishments, or negative consequences, into plans designed to help manage student behaviors.

Table 6.6 Scope and Sequence of Behavioral Skills

Unit 1	Unit 2	Unit 3	Unit 4	Unit 5
Short-term and long-term goal setting • "By the end of the week . . . " • "By the end of the day . . . "	SLANT • **Sit straight** • **Listen actively** • **Ask questions** • **Note key information** • **Track teacher with your eyes**	Respect adults and peers in the classroom • Respectful words • Respectful actions	Using appropriate language in school • Frames • Politeness	Attentive, productive behaviors • Helping peers • Predicting directions

Unit 6	Unit 7	Unit 8	Unit 9	Unit 10
Ready to learn • Environment • Materials • Time	Growth Mindset • Positive self-talk • Comparing to myself	Metacognition • Rehearsal • Elaboration	Self-monitoring • Checking in on my learning • Self-talk and questions	Making connections • To self • To other learning

Punishment affects people in different ways. Imagine a scenario, for example, in which a teacher uses time-out as a behavioral intervention for two students who frequently call out in the classroom. One student stops calling out almost immediately. For this student, time-out is clearly a punisher. The second student persists in calling out, despite being placed repeatedly in time-out. For that student, time-out has no effect and is not a punisher at all. Perhaps this non-responder looks forward to the alone time that this consequence will provide; a time-out is actually meeting the offending student's need.

Punishment is applied at various threshold levels and in various ways by various authority figures. Ensuring consistency by a staff member and between staff members is a necessary goal. Teachers often find punishment to be effective as a classroom behavior management tool, especially in the short term. Because punishment tends to rapidly stop or remove problem behaviors, the teacher, in turn, is positively reinforced for using it (Martens & Meller, 1990). Punishment may appear to be a powerful and attractive behavior management strategy, but may come at a significant cost. Students who are regularly the object of punishment may have less-positive attitudes toward school, as well as poorer attendance and work performance; they may have a more-negative perceptions of teachers and may adopt a more punitive manner in interacting with peers and adults (Martens & Meller, 1990).

Before using any punishment, we should consider whether the student's behavioral problems are caused by a skill deficit. Students should never be punished for behaviors that they cannot help. A student who is chronically disorganized and always arrives late to class with no writing materials may well need to be taught organization skills rather than be punished for lack of preparedness. Positive techniques alone will often adequately improve problem behaviors. We have a range of positive behavior intervention strategies to shape student behaviors as described in Tables 6.1 and 6.3. These positive approaches might include the structuring of the student's classroom experience to avoid behavioral triggers that may lead to problems, or the use of praise and other reinforcers to reward the student for engaging in appropriate behaviors. Punishment techniques, particularly strong forms of punishments such as isolation, should be considered only when the range of positive strategies have not been successful in improving the student's conduct.

Punishment can be effective at changing behaviors when paired with positive reinforcement. The power of punishment techniques is that they can rapidly decrease a student's rate of problem behaviors. But merely suppressing unacceptable behaviors is not enough: the student should also be encouraged to adopt positive classroom behaviors and habits with which to replace negative behavior and habits. Complement negative consequences for inappropriate behaviors with a positive reinforcement system that rewards a child's positive behaviors. Positive reinforcement programs (e.g., sticker chart) should be put into place before using punishments. Only when that positive program begins to show results should a mild punishment component (e.g., response-cost) be added. The best plans use the mildest punishment technique that is likely to be effective. When selecting a punishment technique, start off with less-intensive interventions. Consider moving to a more-intensive or restrictive form of punishment only if the milder alternative proves ineffective. A teacher may first decide to try an in-class time-out (with the student remaining in the classroom during time-out and watching but not otherwise participating in academic activities) before moving to a more-intensive form of isolation time-out in which the student is sent to a special time-out room for misbehavior. In this way, students are not deprived of key opportunities to build social and academic skills.

We must carefully consider possible harmful effects of that consequence before using these negative reinforcers with students. For instance, reducing recess time as a consequence for misbehavior may not be the best approach if the student already has few friends and limited social skills. Similarly, teachers may want to rethink placing students with academic deficits into seclusion time-out or in-school detention, as such a consequence would deprive those children of opportunities for academic instruction that they badly need.

Students should provide input into their behavior plan as it is being developed. One unintended effect of punishment techniques is that the target child may feel powerless, which may erode the child's investment in learning. Giving students a voice in the design of behavior management plans may help students feel empowered. A teacher designing a response-cost plan might ask the student to come up with a secret sign that the teacher might use to signal a warning to the student that he or she is on the verge of having a point deducted from a misbehavior chart.

Teachers and teacher teams, with the support of administrators and support staff, should monitor the effects of the behavior plan, using a procedure such as check-in/check-out described in Chapter 4. Because punishment procedures can in some cases lead to unintended negative effects on student performance and attitudes toward school, behavior plans that include a punishment component should be very closely monitored. Monitoring should include collections of information both about whether the student's problem behaviors are improving under the plan and whether the child is showing any negative reaction to the behavior plan.

Here are some ideas to think about if problems arise when using punishment techniques as part of a larger behavior plan:

• Whenever a new behavior plan is put into place for a student, teachers can expect that the student may initially test the limits of the program. Such testing behavior may include loud complaining or refusing to follow teacher requests. Often, such behaviors subside when the program has been in place and consistently enforced for a short time. If the student reacts to the program with more-serious behavioral outbursts that suggest a safety risk to self or others, the teacher should consider substantially revising or discontinuing the plan immediately. Also, if the student begins to show other negative reactions sometimes associated with use of punishment (e.g., reduced investment in learning, increased hostility toward teaching staff), the teacher should heed these potential warning signs and revise the behavior plan as necessary.

• If a student fails to show significant behavioral improvements within a reasonable amount of time, the teacher should revise or discontinue a plan that contains a punishment component. Teachers should be particularly careful not to regard a behavior plan as effective merely because it makes the student easier to manage. While a teacher may like a time-out intervention because it offers an occasional break from a problem student, that intervention should be regarded as useless or even harmful to the student if it fails to bring about a speedy improvement in that student's behaviors in the classroom.

- It is not uncommon for punishment to lose its effectiveness over time as the recipient of that punishment becomes acclimated to it. In such cases, the problem is usually that the teacher has become overdependent on using punishment techniques alone to manage the student's behaviors.

- A teacher may find that after an intervention has been in place for a month, for instance, that she has to reprimand a student more often and more insistently to get that student to comply with a request. On reflection, the teacher may realize that reprimands have been overused. The teacher may even find reprimands distract other students.

So, what's the final word on punishment or negative reinforcement?

- Use positive reinforcement before negative reinforcement.
- Use positive reinforcement with negative reinforcement.
- Set goals and collect data regarding progress toward goals and adjust the use of punishment if goals are not met.

Tier 3 Behavioral Supports

Tier 2 supports, in the spirit of least-restrictive environment, should reside in the regular classroom, or the Tier 1 core environments, to the maximum extent practical. This is true in behavior just as it is in academics. In academics, Tier 2 interventions support student mastery of the essentials of the grade level or course. The expectation is that teacher teams provide differentiated instruction in these essentials. The same must be true for behaviors. When core instruction in behaviors has been determined to be insufficient for some students, then school teams should provide additional time and different strategies, monitored by a CICO process.

Tier 3 academic supports are typically provided by other staff members, specialists, or assistants, using targeted, intensive strategies, programs, or resources. Tier 3 behavioral supports must follow this design. There exist targeted, research-based behavioral interventions for students who have been diagnosed with intensive needs. These interventions are often low cost or no cost, with the resources and professional development provided by large school districts, county offices of education, area educational agencies, or other regional support groups. Here are a few of these behavioral interventions:

- Project REACH™
- Aggression Replacement Training™
- Nonviolent Crisis Intervention™
- CBITS™

- First Step to Success™
- The Incredible Years™
- Check & Connect™
- Anger Coping Power™

Tiers of Support

Thus, it is entirely possible for a student to receive Tier 1, Tier 2, *and* Tier 3 supports. We do not recommend supplanting access to core content and instruction throughout replacement programs. Consider the following scenario.

Tom is a fifth-grade student. He has failed to pass high-stakes tests in both mathematics and English language arts. A team of staff members, including his grade-level teachers, has diagnosed his reading needs:

- Tom comprehends orally very well. He even shows glimmers of reading comprehension when reading grade-level text, although he reads disfluently and inaccurately. The team believes he is a "word stumbler."
- He reads fifty-six words correct per minute. An error analysis of his reading, confirmed with a phonics diagnostic interview, has revealed patterns of errors with multisyllabic words. He regularly repeats words and phrases. His reading rate decreases the longer he reads.

The team also diagnosed his writing needs:

- Tom has solid ideas but cannot organize them into sentences and paragraphs of a complexity necessary for a fifth grader.
- The voice and word choice of his writing is similarly immature and the fluency of his writing suffers due to lack of transition words and sentence variety.

Tom's mathematics needs were diagnosed as well:

- Tom's mathematical thinking is sound. He can explain, illustrate, and model solutions to problems.
- He can implement the algorithms for multidigit computations with whole numbers, but his math facts make these computations laborious and inaccurate.

In conjunction with the school psychologist and principal, the team also diagnosed Tom's social and academic behavior skills:

- Tom's social behaviors are positive. He attends to instruction, collaborates, works, and plays well with his peers, and responds well to the school's positive behavior plan, which is consistently modeled and reinforced by all teachers with whom Tom works.
- Tom's motivation wanes when presented with complex, multistep tasks. While the school consistently uses an organizational set of steps (read and understand the problem, make a plan, solve the problem, examine your answer), Tom loses steam and stick-with-it-ness when challenges arise.

To meet Tom's needs and help him be successful, the school is providing the following supports:

- Tom's classroom teacher, and the other staff with whom he works, scaffold Tier 1 instruction so he can access core content and demonstrate mastery.
- Access to reading comprehension practice, as well as access to other content's texts, is supported by providing Tom with text within his zone of proximal development (a Tier 1 support). His teachers use their CFAs to monitor his progress.
- Access to content is also supported by providing Tom with audio recordings of texts (a Tier 1 support). His teachers use their CFAs to monitor his progress.
- Tom's writing is supported using sentence and paragraph frames devised, and used consistently, by the school's teachers. He is also provided the option to demonstrate his knowledge orally, using PowerPoint or pictures (a Tier 1 support).
- During small group instruction, Tom's teachers reinforce the Steps to Academic Success with whatever content they are engaged. While this takes time away from the content, Tom and the other students in the group benefit greatly, and there are few extra time periods in the day during which a behavior intervention could be provided (a Tier 2 support). His teacher uses a CICO form to monitor Tom's response to the supplemental support for his motivation and task completion on a daily basis.
- Three days a week, Tom receives thirty minutes of multisyllabic phonics instruction, using REWARDS, from the special education teacher. The multigrade group includes students with and without individualized education program (IEP) plans. The special education teacher monitors and records (with an automatic plotting of data) the progress of her group every two weeks using a multisyllabic pseudo-word assessment.
- Two days a week, Tom receives fluency support for fifteen minutes from an instructional aide, as well as math facts instruction for fifteen minutes on the computer using FASTT Math. Both the phonics and fluency/math facts supports take place during the school's daily thirty-minute flextime. He also practices fluency and math facts with peers while working independently during small group instructional time. The instructional aide monitors and records (with an automatic plotting of data) the progress of her group every two weeks using oral reading fluency and math facts assessments.

The lessons of this scenario could be applied to many other situations. Among other points are these:

- All students have access to the essential academic and behavior content at Tier 1.
- Tiered supports are provided in addition to Tier 1 instruction; they supplement, but do not supplant, core instruction.
- Students receive supports based on their need, not their label.

- Staff provides support based on their expertise, not based on their title or assignment.

In this scenario, we have provided information on *what* scaffolds and interventions that Tom was receiving, the topic of this chapter. We also provided general information on *when* supports are provided and *who* delivers the supports. Specifics on *when* and *who* will be the topic of the next chapter.

SCHOOL CULTURE

- **We don't have the money.**

We recommend that schools inventory the resources they have on site—the human, material, and temporal resources; in other words, we recommend they ask, "How are we using our people, programs, and time?" Every dollar must be considered an instructional dollar. Are we using our money as close to students as possible? This may necessitate hard decisions, but they are decisions we must make. We will not be receiving more money in the near future. We must utilize our dollars in a wiser, more-efficient manner. We can start by reinventorying where our money goes. Moreover, we must examine what we already have, perhaps on shelves or in closets, that we are not utilizing, or due to insufficient training, are not using optimally. In our experiences, we do not have to spend new money for programs; we often have research-based programs that we can reintroduce. Inventory these programs.

In addition, in this chapter we have outlined free ideas and strategies that we can leverage by simply encouraging our staffs to collaborate, investigate, and implement. Whether these resources are found online or lie in the experiences and expertise of our staffs, there are many, many supports that do not require monetary expenditures.

- **We don't have the people.**

In Chapter 7 we will describe options for utilizing staff, but let's reiterate here: *all* staff must enthusiastically collaborate to ensure the success of all students. This includes general education staff, special education staff, English language specialists, reading specialists, and so on, on behalf of general education students with high levels of readiness, general education students with lower levels of readiness, special education students, English learners, and so on. We can rethink the way we use staff; we must, if we are going to meet the differentiated needs of all students.

- **We don't have the time.**

In Chapter 7 we will describe options for inventorying the time available to us and we will share scheduling ideas. But, as is the case with programs (or strategies or interventions) and personnel, we can carve out the time to meet student needs, and we must. The question is whether we have the courage and the will to make hard decisions about how we organize the schedules of staff and students.

- **Some kids just won't get it.**

We now know both neurobiologically, as we have long known behaviorally or experientially, that every student can learn. On the neurobiological front, fMRI (pre- and post-brain scanning) and EEG (brain electrical activity mapping and statistical probability mapping) have revealed that the "appropriate" parts of brains change as a result of high-quality instruction and intervention. Every educator has experienced a student who learns "despite" the most significant obstacles imaginable. Our favorite story is of Christopher, a severely autistic student who was also mute—his parents had never heard him speak coherently. When we last worked with Christopher, he was in a sixth-grade classroom for severely and profoundly disabled students and was reading solidly at a third-grade level. How? It starts with his teacher, Rachel, and involved sign language and a commonly utilized alternative reading program called Edmark.

Yet, even if there remain doubts in some educators' minds regarding the probability that all students can get it, what are our other options? Learning for some students? Which students? Our ethical orientation toward our profession demands that we expect the very best from ourselves and all students at all times. If we do not launch every school year and school day with the firm belief that 100 percent of students will learn at high levels, we are doomed before we have begun.

- **What about punishments or negative consequences?**

We are most certainly not suggesting that students who misbehave, or who fail to meet expectations (such as completing classwork), do not deserve negative consequences. Ensure that such negative consequences are well defined and well communicated to all stakeholders (staff, students, and parents). Ensure that they are consistently applied and that the consequence matches the infraction. Finally, ensure that consequences are communicated to stakeholders in a timely manner. In addition, whenever a consequence is deemed appropriate, do the following:

- Determine if the student possesses the knowledge of the expectations and the skills to meet them.
- Provide reteaching, remediation, or intervention on the skills.
- Identify whether the misbehavior is a symptom of some other need, and problem solve within teams who meet those needs.
- Ensure the student receives positive reinforcement and feedback when expectations are met. Negative reinforcement will not change behaviors; positive reinforcement will modify and solidify behaviors and habits.
- Ensure that the consequence is the consequence. Do not issue the consequence while also humiliating the students in front of their peers.

CHAPTER SUMMARY

We can predict that there will be students who require more time and differentiated supports to learn at high levels. We must be ready. We discussed in Chapter 2 that Tier 2 academic supports should focus on more time and differentiated instructional strategies related to the essentials of the content area or grade level. In Chapter 7 we will discuss when and how these Tier 2 academic supports can be provided.

In this chapter, we described the Tier 3 academic supports, or prescriptions, that follow from the academic diagnostic interviews provided in Chapter 4. We also described the Tier 2 and Tier 3 behavioral supports that follow from the behavioral diagnoses. Possible personnel and scheduling options to provide these interventions will be tackled in Chapter 7.

While we provided detailed resources and strategies for academic and behaviors separately in this chapter, we will have failed if readers have not internalized that academics and behavioral needs must be diagnosed concurrently and supported compatibly. Social and academic behaviors are as critical to college and career readiness as academic skills, and it is rare that an academic or behavioral need exists in isolation; more often, behaviors and academics interact to enhance or derail student success.

In Chapter 7 we will conclude with the system that makes RTI work. We will focus on the *when* and *who* of RTI, as well as the leadership and logistics necessary to ensure that every student graduates high school ready for postsecondary opportunities or a skilled career.

7

Lead the Work With Confidence, Leadership, and Accountability

We cannot expect to achieve the lofty, necessary, and just goals of public education today without acting boldly and differently. High, deep levels of learning, represented by 21st century skills (not broad, shallow knowledge of disjointed skills), for all students (every single student, not simply students with external advantages and internal motivation) will require all educators to enthusiastically accept responsibility for continuous improvement. And educators must be led. What processes will be necessary to fulfill the promises of RTI?

Leadership requires that individuals lead and act. It also requires that others follow. Too often, leaders make decisions without input, without first building shared knowledge, without consensus. Decisions are too often made, and initiatives implemented, without leaders and organizations determining how they will determine the efficacy of initiatives. We cannot continue to make these mistakes. As a start, we must not introduce initiatives until we publicly and specifically identify how we will determine the initiative's success, including by what date, with what data, and using what measure. Most leaders would identify themselves as "change agents" with a capacity to accept and embrace the changes that are seemingly endless in education. Too often, however, the expectation is that others will change when the leader has provided the guidance. This seemingly incongruous approach of "do what I say, not what I do" is a surefire guarantee that the change will not occur. Change becomes rooted and effective in a school or a district only when it becomes "the way we do things around here." As McNulty and Besser (2011, p. 15) point out, "If you want different outcomes, lead differently."

The purpose of this final chapter is to anticipate challenges that school leaders and school principals may face when committing to higher levels of learning for students. A lack of inspired, high-quality leadership is one of the most pressing problems for public education. School leadership can and must improve. Before predicting some of the challenges school leaders may face, let's first explore evidence-based strategies and ideas that all great leaders employ.

GENERAL PRINCIPLES OF LEADERSHIP

Effective leadership practices translate across different types of organizations. Jim Collins' supplement to *Good to Great* (2001), published as a monogram for social sectors including educational institutions, illustrates this point. The characteristics of great organizations in *Good to Great*, and the two nearly identical studies that preceded it, *In Search of Excellence*, by Tom Peters and Robert Waterman (1982), and *Built to Last*, by Collins and Tom Porras (1994), are listed in the first three columns of Table 7.1. Elaine McEwan in *Seven Steps to Effective Instructional Leadership* (2003); Robert Marzano, Timothy Waters, and Brian McNulty in *School Leadership That Works* (2005); and Rick DuFour and Marzano in *Leaders of Learning* (2011) draw on their research of best practices and extensive experiences to describe the characteristics of effective school leaders. These characteristics are listed in the last three columns of Table 7.1. The purpose of the table is to

- suggest that we already know the best ideas regarding how to lead schools that ensure high levels of student learning;
- confirm that the research-based best leadership practices in other industries match the research-based best leadership practices in education;
- demonstrate that there are a definable set of attributes of great leaders and organizations; and
- articulate that these attributes are more often simple than complex.

What can we summarize and glean from the table of the most effective organizational and leadership practices (Table 7.1)? How do these lessons apply to principals and other school leaders? How do these attributes apply to challenges that we can predict that leaders will face? First, a synthesis of these studies:

- Lead from the front. Get out of the office, ask questions, and listen. Leaders are doers, and they must serve their stakeholders.
- People make the organization great. No program exists that will solve all the phonemic awareness, phonics, comprehension, writing, mathematics, or behavioral challenges that students may have. It is people—valued, supported, trained, and led—who will transform public education.

Table 7.1 Best Practices in Leadership in Industry and Education

In Search of Excellence	Built to Last	Good to Great	Seven Steps to Effective Instructional Leadership	School Leadership That Works	Leaders of Learning
• Autonomy and entrepreneurship • Hands-on, value-driven	• Home-grown management • Cult-like cultures	• Level 5 leadership	• Maintain positive attitudes toward students, staff, and parents • Create a school culture and climate conducive to learning	• Affirmation • Change agent • Ideas/beliefs	• Leadership is an affair of the heart • Create the collaborative culture of a professional learning community
• Productivity through people • Simple form, lean staff • Close to the customer		• First who, then what	• Develop teacher leaders • Be there for your staff	• Monitoring/evaluating • Intellectual stimulation • Visibility • Relationships • Resources • Situational awareness	• School improvement means people improvement
• Stick to the knitting	• Preserve the core/stimulate progress • Clock building, not time telling	• Hedgehog concept • The Flywheel		• Order • Knowledge of curriculum, instruction, and assessment	• Ensuring effective instruction

(Continued)

Table 7.1 (Continued)

In Search of Excellence	Built to Last	Good to Great	Seven Steps to Effective Instructional Leadership	School Leadership That Works	Leaders of Learning
• Simultaneous loose-tight properties	• The end of the beginning • Good enough never is	• Culture of discipline • Confront the brutal facts	• Establish and implement instructional goals	• Discipline • Culture • Focus • Input	
• A bias for action	• Try a lot of stuff and keep what works	• Technology accelerators		• Optimizer • Involvement in curriculum, instruction, and assessment	• Developing a guaranteed and viable curriculum • Responding when kids don't learn
• Managing ambiguity and paradox	• No "tyranny of the OR" (embrace the "genius of the AND")		• Communicate the vision and mission of your school	• Communication • Outreach • Flexibility	
	• Big hairy audacious goals		• Set high expectations for your staff	• Contingent rewards	• Ongoing monitoring of student learning

- Be honest and have courageous conversations. The job of educating students at the very highest levels is too important and challenging to allow people or practices to languish.
- Be focused! Create focus! We most certainly suffer from initiative-fatigue. There may be no silver bullets, but asking and expecting staffs to successfully execute dozens of new initiatives, or a new initiative every year, is a guaranteed way of spiraling toward failure. Our Law of Initiative Fatigue suggests that when resources of time, money, and emotional energy are held constant while the number of old, continuing, and new initiatives rises, organizational implosion is inevitable.
- Determine what is nonnegotiable and why, and then allow staff the opportunity to make expectations happen. Leaders must create clarity and shared knowledge regarding the truly important elements of schooling and instruction. Once established, stick to these themes, and avoid micromanaging.
- Ready, fire, aim—students don't have time for us to perpetuate the knowing-doing gap. If we wait until we know precisely what plagues a student or until we have the perfect support, the student will have fallen farther behind. Instead, let's recognize that we learn so much through the process of intervening and that our first, intensive efforts may meet a student's needs.
- Embrace continuous learning. We will never be done, challenges will always exist, and they will change. That's one of the reasons that the profession is so gratifying.
- The world is not binary. We can and must embrace the "genius of the AND" (Collins, 2001). There are no perfect, or perfectly effective, ideas. We must accept that concepts such as phonics and whole language are both essential for high levels of student learning.
- The higher our expectations, the higher our results. There's a correlation. Culture is more important than structures. Our attitudes toward and belief in every student will transfer to students' belief in themselves.
- Educators must utilize every resource as close to the students as possible. Schools exist first and foremost to ensure that all students are equipped to succeed after graduating from high school, to be contributing members of our society. When dollars are scarce and decisions must be made about where to deploy resources, we must ensure that these resources are used as efficiently as possible in the effort to meet every student's needs and improve every student's life chances.

These are the characteristics of great schools and great leaders as suggested in the literature from industry and education. How might we apply these characteristics to challenges that school leaders may face?

Leadership Challenges to Transforming Education

The challenges facing us, and the opportunities available to us, are profound and long lasting. If we ensure that every student stays on track to be a critically thinking, problem-solving, literate, and numerate citizen every step of the way, each student's success and the very nature of schools and schooling will be profoundly and positively impacted. This is truly a golden opportunity and one that we have too often missed up to this point. This may be because of the very real challenges that exist. How can we apply the lessons of effective organizations to a few of the challenges that we can expect?

Establishing, Organizing, and Monitoring Systems of Support

We can predict that despite our best efforts some students will experience difficulties that require interventions. We cannot be surprised by these developments and must be ready to provide supports immediately on identifying these students. Furthermore, screening to identify the needs of these students must occur frequently, perhaps even more frequently than the three times a year that is the norm. These are the fundamental premises of the framework known as RTI. If it's predictable, it's preventable.

Who should be primarily responsible for establishing, organizing, and monitoring systems of support; in other words, who on school campuses should lead RTI efforts? The answer is simple and essential—site principals. There is not a more significant role for the principal than leading these efforts. Principals must lead. They must work with staff to schedule when supports will occur. They must work with staff to organize personnel and materials. And they must be the primary individual responsible for gathering, analyzing, and utilizing data.

Simply stated, principals must be in meetings—leading, facilitating, and/or significantly contributing to meetings. They should be in classrooms, observing instruction; in intervention sessions, encouraging students; in hallways and resource rooms, assessing students to monitor their progress; on the computer, analyzing the progress of students. They must lead; effective leaders lead through actions and they lead from the front.

RTI Team Decision Making

While the outcomes for students within special education have been alarming, the primary reason for using caution when providing students ever-increasing supports is that we have an ethical (and legal) obligation to provide students with appropriate supports, supports that will result in rapid rates of progress, in the least restrictive environment possible. To ensure that teams make the best decisions on behalf of students, we recommend that staff follow a decision-making protocol similar to the one below:

Is the student responding to intervention? What is the rate of improvement?

- The rate is adequate.
  - The target has been met.
  - The progress will be sustained.
  - Discontinue intervention, document date, and continue to monitor.

- More time is needed to solidify progress.
  - o Continue intervention and document date.
- The target has not been met.
  - o Continue intervention and document date.

OR

- The rate is inadequate. (Document any changes and record date.)
  - o The student's behavior is a concern.
  - o Examine concerns with attention, motivation, attendance, or socialization.
  - o Diagnose antecedents to misbehavior.
  - o Involve the social worker and other clinicians.
  - o Use CICO with fidelity, with a mentor, and with acknowledgments for appropriate behaviors.
  - o Consider adjusting duration of each support.
  - o Consider adjusting the frequency of supports.
  - o Consider adjusting the group size.
  - o Consider using a more appropriate progress monitoring probe.
  - o Ensure the intervention is at the student's current instructional level.
  - o Consider providing a more targeted intervention.
  - o Consider providing more PD for the interventionist.
  - o Better differentiate and support the student in the regular classroom.

Teams must follow consistent protocols when revising supports for students at risk.

RTI and Leadership Pitfalls

The basic tenets of RTI (universal screening, universal quality instruction, frequent formative assessment and descriptive feedback, catching behavior and academic problems early, and intentional follow-up) are part of any school vision and are key to the work of successful leaders. When they are further enhanced through strong collaborative teams should "seal the deal" and ensure improved student outcomes. Yet, there are pitfalls. DuFour and Marzano (2011), whose work is referenced in Table 7.1, outline ten common mistakes schools and districts make as they embark on building a foundation of RTI. Inevitably, they are traced back to the role of the leader. We've adapted their list here:

1. Add-on RTI. If teachers teach without checking whether or not students are learning and assessment becomes the tool for ranking and sorting students, then intervention will have little impact. If instead intervention is integrated within the context of a guaranteed and viable curriculum, regular formative assessment, and ongoing improvement, *all* students will show gains.

2. Checklist RTI. If RTI is viewed as a fad or represented by a purchased program, the school will fail to develop an effective intervention plan. Implementing RTI to meet a mandate of compliancy will not lead to improvement. Effective implementation leads to RTI being "the way we do things around here."

3. Reactive RTI. If the approach is to "wait and see" where students are in terms of behavior and academics, it's likely too late to intervene in an effective fashion. The educational autopsy yields less valuable information than the educational physical.

4. Replacement RTI. If students are removed from "regular" classroom instruction for reading to be placed in the "special" classroom instruction for reading, they may get different strategies but not additional time. Similarly, if students are given more time but not a different instructional approach, they are also not receiving effective intervention. Students require both differentiated instructional strategies *and* time to bridge the gaps. These are the same recommendations that Benjamin Bloom made in the 1960s under the guise of Mastery Learning (1968).

5. RTI on demand. Inviting students to drop by during unstructured time (before school, at lunch, or after school) as needed will not ensure that students most at risk receive timely and frequent interventions. RTI must be mandatory.

6. Timed RTI. If a formula existed that defined intervention in terms of seat time, we would all be using it. If the objective is proficiency, time will not drive decisions.

7. Generalized RTI. When intervention is assigned on the basis of a general concern ("Chris failed math") rather than a specific struggle ("Chris has difficulty with regrouping when subtracting four-digit numbers"), the effectiveness of supplemental supports will be limited.

8. Private RTI. If the approach to intervention does not include widespread communication with all stakeholders who contribute to the process, including their roles and responsibilities and a systematic plan, RTI will be ineffective.

9. Untrained RTI. Too frequently students who need the most-skilled teachers do not get them. Instead, education assistants, volunteers, or new teachers, with a wide variation in their teaching load, provide intervention. Too often, the result is a widening of the learning gap.

10. RTI = special education. RTI is intended as a universal approach that strengthens instruction for *all* students in order to preserve special education for those who have identified physical or mental disabilities. This will allow our highly trained special educators to serve the children for which special education was designed.

LEADING SCHOOLS FOR THE 21ST CENTURY

It is possible and necessary to both ensure that students have a rock-solid basis in literacy and numeracy and that students engage in critical thinking and problem solving. People make the organization great and people can ensure that both these goals are met. Achieving this dual goal will require honest and courageous conversations. The world is not binary. It is possible to create learning experiences that merge art, critical thinking, collaboration, and literacy. It is possible to create learning experiences that merge games, problem solving, cooperation, and numeracy. It will not be easy, but it will be made possible by focusing the scope of content, particularly in literacy and numeracy. School leaders must give teachers the permission and the time to focus the overly broad curriculum that state standards and textbooks have traditionally (ill) defined.

Addressing the Common Refrains

How often have educators uttered these words about students: "They will catch up next year" or "They're not mature enough" or "They're not developmentally ready." This is often the case for our youngest learners, and yet the National Reading Panel and National Mathematics Advisory Panel both address misconceptions about the capabilities of children in Kindergarten. Success for young children is much more individualized and based more on prior experiences than it is on innate developmental readiness. In allowing time for students to "catch up," we have passed on problems to teachers at future grade levels and seriously compromised students' futures. We should know better. The realities and rigor of schooling will inevitably and unfortunately lead to students who are behind in Kindergarten and first grade being seriously at risk in second and third grade. Yes, students may catch up in their phonemic awareness and phonics abilities, but while they have been struggling to access connected text, their peers have been independently reading, building a substantial reservoir of vocabulary and background knowledge, and a prowess at comprehending and making meaning. Geoffrey Canada, CEO of the Harlem Children's Zone, shared his view of this conundrum: "If we do the same for all students every year, we should not expect individual change. If a student is two years behind another student and we give them both a year of school, what do we see at the end of the year?" (author's notes, paraphrased from a recent address). The answer, of course, is that we see no change in the previously identified gap.

What makes the refrains of low expectations even more dangerous is the fact that students from environments of socioeconomic disadvantage often come to school already thousands of words behind their peers (National Institute of Child Health and Human Development, 2000). Leaders must be vociferous and consistent in their message that every student can and will learn at the very highest levels. When schools identify students as behind, they must make supports available for them the very next day. If these students respond quickly to these immediate supports, if it turns out that they simply needed a little time to acclimatize to the demands of school, all the better. Effective leaders—and effective schools—ensure that developmental readiness, maturity, socialization, and behavior are not used as excuses but rather as variables that can be influenced. If behaviors, for example, are contributing to difficulties in learning letter sounds, then both behavior and letter sounds are addressed. There is no delay in intervening. There is no lowering of expectations for all.

Resist the Temptation to Focus on Upper Grades

Many schools have succumbed to the temptation to focus resources on the grades constituting the graduation program because of the threat of sanctions. The structural implications of focusing only on upper grades are serious. First, if the causes of student difficulties in upper grades—namely insufficient supports and/or rigor in primary grades—are not addressed, then the reactionary practices of upper grade remediation will always exist. Second, schools that focus on remediating skills in upper grades will likely not be as focused on improving the quality of core instruction in all grades. The best solution is neither remediation in the upper grades *nor* preventative supports in the primary grades, but for schools to embrace the genius of AND. We certainly must address the needs of students at risk in all grade levels. This is a moral imperative. But principals and school leaders must also lead staffs in focusing and improving their core craft. Leaders must collaboratively define the true raison d'être of schools and then trust and support their staff in achieving these high expectations.

One more thing: practically speaking, students at risk in early grades will likely respond to supports much more quickly than students in upper grades (Weber, 2013) because skills are more discrete and younger students have not had time to fall as far behind. Wise leaders will leverage this potential success, communicating and proclaiming to all that students and staff at the school can and will be wildly successful when work is focused and expectations are high. Primary grade successes have the ability to transform cultures and contribute to simultaneous successes in upper grades. Have the courage to ask why all students cannot be successful. Confront biases and stereotypes. Lead with passion and a sense of social justice. Our beliefs in ourselves and in students are powerful levers for improvement.

Identifying Time, Human, and Material Resources

There are undoubtedly other challenges that principals and school leaders may face, but the last challenge on which this chapter will focus is the understandable but unproductive excuse that we do not possess the time or resources to do our job. Principals and school leaders themselves often express this refrain, and this must change. Leaders must convey the belief that we can and will meet the needs of all students given the resources we currently possess. What makes this message easier to proclaim is that it's true. There are schools in your city, state, province, as well as in the nation and world, that are having success with the same amount of time and the same levels of resources. It's not a lack of time, resource, or even skill that is preventing us from realizing schools' and students' potentials; it's often a lack of will. Sample schedules in Table 7.2 give some idea of how an elementary school or a high school might build in the time necessary for intervention and collaboration.

As for the content of the collaborative conversations that can lead to these schedules, Table 7.3 has some suggestions.

Let's start changing the conversations about resources by collaboratively determining what is nonnegotiable and why. Regularly revisit this conversation

Table 7.2 Schedule Examples

High School

Monday and Wednesday		Tuesday and Thursday		Friday	
Period 0	6:50–7:55	Period 0	6:50–7:55	Collaboration	7:45–8:50
Period 1	8:00–9:40	Period 2	8:00–9:40	Period 1	9:00–9:48
Interventions	9:40–10:00	Interventions	9:40–10:00	Period 2	9:54–10:42
Break	10:00–10:10	Break	10:00–10:10	Break	10:42–10:51
Period 3	10:15–11:55	Period 4	10:15–11:55	Period 3	10:57–11:45
Interventions	11:55–12:15	Interventions	11:55–12:15	Period 4	11:51–12:39
Lunch	12:15–12:45	Lunch	12:15–12:45	Lunch	12:39–1:09
Period 5	12:50–2:30	Period 6	12:50–2:30	Period 5	1:15–2:03
Interventions	2:30–2:50	Interventions	2:30–2:50	Period 6	2:09–2:57

Elementary School

Content	Time
ELA	8:00–10:00
Recess	10:05–10:20
Math	10:25–11:25
English language development	11:30–12:00
Lunch	12:05–12:40
Social studies/science	12:45–1:25
Physical education	1:30–1:50
Intervention/enrichment Block 1	1:55–2:25
Special/elective	2:30–3:00

Table 7.3 Suggested Schedule Content

Prioritize Content	Analyzer Time Blocks	Intervention/Enrichment Block
• Just as we prioritize standards within content, rank the most critical content . . . content that students cannot miss. • Tier 2 and 3 interventions should be provided (reluctantly, temporarily, and flexibly) in place of lesser-prioritized content.	• Where might there be inefficiencies in the schedule (e.g., transitions, lunch)? • Which support staff (transportation, food services, etc.) can be brought into the dialogue to expand opportunities to provide learning opportunities?	• When within the existing start and dismissal times could a 30-minute block be inserted? • Could it be provided in common for grade/content teams?

and then ensure folks make it happen. Next, inventory your time, human, and material resources. A great activity for all staff is to look at what is currently on hand. A scavenger hunt of current material resources always reveals some nuggets that can be put to good use. Many storage rooms in schools in which we have worked have revealed quality items that were either minimally used or, on occasion, completely unused. Staff can quickly and easily inventory items currently on hand before determining what needs to be acquired elsewhere. Regarding time, examine how much more time may be captured if lunch periods are combined between grade levels or separated within grade levels. Pull apart the "master schedule" and ensure that it is optimally organized. It won't be easy, and some staff may have to change the way they've always done things, but it can be done. Determine how instruction can consistently start closer to the beginning of class and continue closer to the end, and then hold one another accountable for maximizing the available instructional time. Table 7.4 shows a schedule for a staff member who specializes in intervention. Notice the structured and unstructured components of the schedule. Awareness of these blocks may help to identify when this valuable individual can further assist the classroom environment.

Marzano (2003) long ago found that we utilize only about 50 percent of class time for learning. Table 7.5 shows an example of how one high school managed to create extra time prior to the end of each reporting period so students could catch up on missed assignments, receive remediation or extension activities, or plan for upcoming work. Initially billed as a one-time event each quarter, the outcomes were so positive that staff asked the principal to consider making the schedule adjustment more regular and especially during those weeks when a non-school day fell on a Monday or Friday.

Regarding human resources, inventory where paraprofessionals and specialists work every minute of the day. Could their time be better focused so it more directly impacts students and student learning? Their jobs typically span multiple teachers, grade levels, and content areas. A big-picture point of view is necessary when scheduling their days, and there is little margin for inefficiencies. In some K–8 schools, sixth-, seventh-, and eighth-grade

Table 7.4   Intervention Specialist Schedule

Times	Grade Level(s)	Students	Content Focus	Program	Location
8:00–8:30	6		Phonics	Rewards	Room 212
8:30–9:00	6–8		Fluency	Six-Minute Solution	Room 212
9:00–9:30	6		Comprehension	Making Connections	Room 212
9:30–10:00	7		Phonics	Rewards	Room 212
10:00–11:00	Preparation Time				
11:00–11:30	7		Comprehension	Making Connections	Room 310
11:30–12:00	6–8		Fluency	Six-Minute Solution	Room 310
12:00–12:30	Lunch Time				
12:30–1:00	6		Math	IXL.com	Room 310
1:00–1:30	7		Math	IXL.com	Room 310
1:30–2:00	8		Comprehension	Making Connections	Room 310
2:00–2:30	Progress Monitoring Time				
2:30–3:00	6–8		Fluency	Six-Minute Solution	Room 310

Note: IXL.com is an online collection of math questions that provides simple reteaching when items are answered incorrectly.

Table 7.5   Intervention Week Timetable Adjustments

Monday	Tuesday	Wednesday	Thursday	Friday
Period 2	Period 3	Period 1	Period 4	Period 1
Break	Break	Break	Break	Break
Period 1	Period 4	Period 2	Period 3	Period 2
Period 1 Extended	Period 4 Extended	Period 2 Extended	Period 3 Extended	
Lunch	Lunch	Lunch	Lunch	Lunch
Period 4	Period 1	Period 3	Period 2	Period 3
Period 3	Period 2	Period 4	Period 1	Period 4

teachers have agreed to give up one preparatory period a week to intervene with students in Kindergarten and first grade. In another school, the principal's secretary declared that the half-hour after lunch was often quiet and asked to lead a reading group during that time. In still another school, the building custodian agreed to lead a weekly upper-grade literature circle for students in need of enrichment. The job of educating children is the most important in the world, and it has become more daunting and critical. If we do not commit to thinking and behaving differently, we should not expect or hope for different outcomes.

Regarding material resources, we can undeniably state that we have access to free reading resources that can meet most of the needs of students in all grade levels. The first dose of intervention, and perhaps the best form of support, is based on identifying specific skills with which students have had difficulty, diagnosing causal reasons for difficulty, and reteaching in a smaller group with alternate strategies, with support provided by the staff member with the greatest skill set for the job. We specifically addressed this important topic in Chapter 5.

More resources need not mean more money. In fact, the first and best solutions, whether in response to time, human, or material resources, are not at all dependent on dollars. Every resource must be utilized as close to students as possible. And, after inventorying resources, we must not delay action. Ready, fire, aim is not an inappropriate principle. The medical model, so popular to apply to education, applies here too; through a process of diagnose-prescribe-diagnose-prescribe, we will successfully ensure all students learn at high levels. A commitment to continuous learning is both a desired cultural norm and a practical necessity.

Oftentimes we hear of the need to "think outside the box" as a creative process that will lead to a solution to the challenges schools face. This quest for a panacea is doomed to fail if the quest begins without a firm knowledge of what exists inside the box—the very school in which you are working. Perhaps a starting point might be to create an inventory of staff members' skills and availabilities. This can be followed by identifying which *staff* members can be prepared to provide which *supports* at which *times*. Further analysis might help to specify the area of possible deficits in student learning for which the school currently possesses strategies, materials, resources, and programs and, conversely, to identify the areas of possible deficits where the school *does not* currently possess strategies, materials, resources, and programs. At the end of the day, "outside the box" thinking is really "inside the box" thinking; at the very least, all thinking begins inside the box, where we currently are. In achieving this understanding, we may find that the solutions we need are close at hand.

SCHOOL CULTURE

Some areas of leadership that will be impacted in the culture conversation include the following:

- **I need full buy-in to move this RTI work forward.**

    This refrain speaks to the uncertainty for leaders as to whether the work is worth the effort required. The more knowledgeable leaders become, the easier it becomes to craft a response to this concern. We are well aware of the myriad demands on leaders' time. We are equally aware of the significant impact that attending meetings, reading texts, and cocreating solutions with their respective staffs have on this critical work. As with any group of individuals, some staff members will be early adopters, others will need time to process the change, and a smaller group will be from the "show-me" camp. While desirable to have anyone on the "same page," occasionally leaders need to indicate "what book we're in" and when we'll be "completing each chapter." Put more succinctly, sometimes leaders need to lead. This is offered in the most respectful manner; we know it's necessary to offer complete support to those struggling as the school moves in a new and challenging direction.

• **I lead by committee and think a distributed leadership model works best.**

As alluded to throughout this text, it is necessary to have all staff understand the *why* of this work and the direction in which the school is headed. Using data as evidence to define the route and frequently checking in (and celebrating successes) keeps the objectives clear in the minds of all. When distributed leadership is operationalized as collaborative work between individuals who trust and respect each other's contribution, it aligns with having "all hands on deck" and contributes to the overall goal, without the leader needing to oversee each aspect of the work. If instead distributed leadership is used to disguise power differentials or to avoid more consultative leadership practices, it becomes the beginning of the death knell for RTI (or any well-intentioned initiative that needs collective support).

CHAPTER SUMMARY

The active leadership of school principals and other site leaders is essential to ensuring greater levels of success for students and staff and greater outcomes for schools. For an effective RTI program to take hold in a school, it must be fully supported by the school leadership team. RTI must become part of what a school believes, and it must be communicated that RTI will lead to better outcomes for all students. We possess the knowledge of what strategies and frameworks will result in success. We know that curricular and instructional dogmas work well for some but that balanced approaches are more sensible and successful. We know that interventions in isolation will result in little change but the same interventions operating as part of an integrated approach have the potential to raise the level of student achievement. We know that cultures are more important than structures, and that cultures are created and cocreated by leaders. As Schlechty (1997, 136) states, "Structural change that is not supported by cultural change will eventually be overwhelmed by the culture, for it is in the culture that the organization finds meaning and stability." The questions do not concern the "knowing" aspect of our work—they concern the "doing" part of our work. Effective, involved, supportive leadership is the key to closing that gap. "Every action a prominent school leader takes demonstrates his or her priorities and belief system" (Reason, 2010, p. 13).

Epilogue

The Next Steps

We began this book imploring readers to consider "why" the education profession should change a system that has seemingly worked for as long as our schools have been in existence. This book presents answers to the "why" and "how" questions of school improvement and RTI, answers necessary in our schools to ensure *all* students graduate from high school ready for postsecondary success or a skilled career.

Our evolving knowledge of students and student needs allows us to meet them where they are and support them in progressing to where they must be. Responding with the appropriate interventions, identified using the assessment tools discussed (screening tool, progress monitoring checks, and diagnostics) will allow students to achieve positive outcomes. They will also allow teachers to do what they do best—teach and instill a love of learning.

RTI is a verb. It demands action on the part of every educator on behalf of every student. It requires a shift in our conversations, from talking about *my* students to talking about *all* students. In order to assist educators in ensuring that children overcome the dire outcomes that socio-economic factors would seemingly predict, we've proposed a series of strategies and tools that are practical to apply. It is our sincere hope that these strategies and tools will help shift conversations away from using factors outside of school as excuses and, instead, use them as sources of information that will provide insights for more strategically and urgently designed systems of support.

References

Adams, M. J., Foorman, B. R., Lundberg, I., & Beeler, T. (1998). *Phonemic awareness in young children.* Baltimore, MD: Paul H. Brookes.

Ainsworth, L. (2003a). *Power Standards: Identifying the standards that matter most.* Englewood, CO: Lead + Learn Press.

Ainsworth, L. (2003b). *"Unwrapping" the standards: A simple process to make standards manageable.* Englewood, CO: Lead + Learn Press.

Ainsworth, L. (2010). *Rigorous curriculum design: How to create curricular units of study that align standards, instruction, and assessment.* Englewood, CO: Lead + Learn Press.

Alliance for Excellent Education. (2008). *The high cost of high school dropouts: What the nation pays for inadequate high schools.* Washington, DC: Author.

Anderson, J. R. (2000). *Learning and memory: An integrated approach.* New York: John Wiley & Sons.

Bandura, A. (1977). *Social Learning Theory.* Englewood Cliffs, NJ: Prentice Hall.

Barth, R. S. (2001). *Learning by heart.* San Francisco: Jossey-Bass.

Beck, I. L., McKeown, M. G., & Kucan, L. (2002). *Bringing words to life: Robust vocabulary instruction.* New York: Guilford Press.

Benson, J. (2012). 100 repetitions. *Educational Leadership, 70*(2), 76–78.

Bloom, B. S. (1968). Learning for mastery. *Evaluation Comment, 1*(2), 1–12.

Bloom, B. S. (1984). The search for methods of group instruction as effective as one-to-one tutoring. *Educational Leadership,* 5–17.

Boynton, M., & Boynton, C. (2005). *The educator's guide to preventing and solving discipline problems.* Alexandria, VA: Association for Supervision and Curriculum Development.

Braithwaite, R. (2001). *Managing aggression.* New York: Routledge.

Brock, S. E. (1998). Helping the student with ADHD in the classroom: Strategies for teachers. *Communiqué, 26*(5), 18–20.

Buffum, A., Mattos, M., & Weber, C. (2009). *Pyramid response to intervention: RtI, PLCs, and how to respond when students don't learn.* Bloomington, IN: Solution Tree Press.

Buffum, A., Mattos, M., & Weber, C. (2010). The why behind RTI. *Educational Leadership, 68*(2), 10–16.

Buffum, A., Mattos, M., & Weber, C. (2011). *Simplifying response to intervention: Four essential guiding principles.* Bloomington, IN: Solution Tree Press.

Carnevale, A. (2001). *Help wanted . . . college required.* ETS Leadership 2000 Series. Princeton, NJ: Educational Testing Service.

Carnine, D. W. (1976). Effects of two teacher presentation rates on off-task behavior, answering correctly, and participation. *Journal of Applied Behavior Analysis, 9,* 199–206.

Carroll, T. (2009). The next generation of learning teams. *Phi Delta Kappan, 91*(2), 8–13.

Collins, J. (2001). *Good to great: Why some companies make the leap . . . and others don't.* New York: HarperCollins.

Collins, J. C., & Porras, J. I. (1994). *Built to last: Successful habits of visionary companies.* New York: HarperCollins.

Conley, D. T. (2010). *College and career ready: Helping all students succeed beyond high school.* San Francisco: Jossey-Bass.

Covington, M. V. (1997). *Self-worth and motivation.* New York: Cambridge University Press.

Cronin, J., Dahlin, M., Adkins, D., & Kingsbury, G. G. (2007). *The proficiency illusion.* Washington, DC: Thomas B. Fordham Institute.

Cronin, J., Kingsbury, G. G., Dahlin, M., & Bowe, B. (2007). *Alternate methodologies for estimating state standards on a widely used computer adaptive test.* Paper presented at the American Educational Research Association, Chicago.

DuFour, R. (2011). Work together but only if you want to. *Kappan 92*(5), 57–61.

DuFour, R., DuFour, R., Eaker, R., & Many, T. (2011). *Learning by doing.* Bloomington, IN: Solution Tree Press.

DuFour, R., & Marzano, R. J. (2011). *Leaders of learning: How district, school, and classroom leaders improve student achievement.* Bloomington, IN: Solution Tree Press.

Duke, N. K., & Pearson, P. D. (2002). Effective practices for developing reading comprehension. In A. E. Farstup & S. J Samuels (Eds.), *What research has to say about reading instruction* (pp. 205–242). Newark, DE: International Reading Association.

DuPaul, G. J., & Ervin, R. A. (1996). Functional assessment of behaviors related to attention-deficit/hyperactivity disorder: Linking assessment to intervention design. *Behavior Therapy, 27,* 601–622.

DuPaul, G. J., & Stoner, G. (2003). *ADHD in the schools: Assessment and intervention strategies* (2nd ed.). New York: Guilford.

Dweck, C. S. (2006). *Mindset: The new psychology of success.* New York: Random House.

Edmonds, R. (1979). Effective schools for the urban poor. *Educational Leadership, 37*(1), 15–24.

Fisher, D., & Frey, N. (2008). *Better learning through structured teaching: A framework for the gradual release of responsibility.* Alexandria, VA: Association for Supervision and Curriculum Development.

Ford, A. D., Olmi, D. J., Edwards, R. P., & Tingstrom, D. H. (2001). The sequential introduction of compliance training components with elementary-aged children in general education classroom settings. *School Psychology Quarterly, 16,* 142–157.

Fullan, M. (2006). *Turnaround leadership.* San Francisco: Jossey-Bass.

Gersten, R., & Chard, D. J. (1999). Number sense: Rethinking arithmetic instruction for students with mathematical disabilities. *Journal of Special Education, 33,* 18–28.

Gersten, R., Clarke, B., Haymond, K., & Jordan, N. (2011). *Screening for mathematics difficulties in K–3 students* (2nd ed.). Portsmouth, NH: RMC Research Corporation, Center on Instruction.

Gettinger, M. (1988). Methods of proactive classroom management. *School Psychology Review, 17,* 227–242.

Gettinger, M., & Seibert, J. K. (2002). Best practices in increasing academic learning time. In A. Thomas (Ed.), *Best practices in school psychology IV* (4th ed., Vol. I, pp. 773–787). Bethesda, MD: National Association of School Psychologists.

Ginsburg, A., Leinwand, S., Anstrom, T., & Pollock, E. (2005). *What the United States can learn from Singapore's world-class mathematics system (and what Singapore can learn from the United States): An exploratory study.* Washington, DC: American Institutes for Research.

Goleman, D. (2006). *Social intelligence: The new science of human relationships*. New York: Bantam Dell.

Gonzales, P., Williams, T., Jocelyn, L., Roey, S., Kastberg, D., and Brenwald, S. (2008). *Highlights From TIMSS 2007: Mathematics and Science Achievement of US Fourth- and Eighth-Grade Students in an International Context* (NCES 2009–001 Revised). Washington, DC: U.S. Department of Education.

Guskey, T. R. (2007). Closing achievement gaps: Revisiting Benjamin S. Bloom's "Learning for Mastery." *Journal of Advanced Academics. 19*, 8–31.

Hamre, B. K., & Pianta, R. C. (2005). Can instructional and emotional support in the first-grade classroom make a difference for children at risk of school failure? *Child Development, 76*(5), 949–967.

Hanushek, E. A., Peterson, P. E., & Woessmann, L. (2011). Teaching math to the talented: Which countries—and states—are producing high-achieving students? *Education Next 11*(1), 10–18.

Hattie, J. (2009). *Visible learning: A synthesis of over 800 meta-analyses relating to student achievement*. New York: Routledge.

Heward, W. L. (1994). Three "low-tech" strategies for increasing the frequency of active student response during group instruction. In R. Gardner III, D. M. Sainato, J. O. Cooper, T. E. Heron, W. L. Heward, J. Eshleman, & T. A. Grossi (Eds.), *Behavior analysis in education: Focus on measurably superior instruction* (pp. 283–320). Monterey, CA: Brooks/Cole.

Hierck, T., Coleman, C., & Weber, C. (2011). *Pyramid of behavior interventions: Seven keys to a positive learning environment*. Bloomington, IN: Solution Tree Press.

Hirsch, E. D. Jr. (2006). The case for bringing content into the language arts block and for a knowledge-rich curriculum core for all children. *American Educator, 30*(1).

Hollingsworth, J., & Ybarra, S. (2009). *Explicit direction instruction (EDI): The power of the well-crafted, well-taught lesson*. Thousand Oaks, CA: Corwin.

Hook, P. E., & Jones, S. D. (2004). The importance of automaticity and fluency for efficient reading comprehension. *Perspectives on Language and Literacy, 28*(1), 9–14.

Hunter, M. (1982). *Mastery teaching*. El Segundo, CA: TIP Publications.

Jacobs, H. H. (1997). *Mapping the big picture: Integrating curriculum and assessment K–12*. Alexandria, VA: Association of Supervision and Curriculum Development.

Kalchman, M., Moss, J., & Case, R. (2001). Psychological models for the development of mathematical understanding: Rational numbers and functions. In S. Carver & D. Klahr (Eds.), *Cognition and Instruction* (pp. 1–38). Mahwah, NJ: Lawrence Erlbaum Associates.

Kazdin, A. E. (1989). *Behavior modification in applied settings* (4th ed.). Pacific Grove, CA: Brooks/Cole.

Kuhl, J., & Atkinson, J. W. (1986). *Motivation, thought, and action*. New York: Praeger Publishers.

Lamon, S. J. (2007). Rational numbers and proportional reasoning: Toward a theoretical framework for research. In F. K. Lester, Jr. (Ed.), *Second handbook of research on mathematics teaching and learning* (pp. 629–668). National Council of Teachers of Mathematics, Charlotte, NC: Information Age Publishing.

Lanceley, F. J. (1999). *On-scene guide for crisis negotiators*. Boca Raton, FL: CRC Press.

Lezotte, L. W. (1991). *Correlates of effective schools: The first and second generations*. Okemos, MI: Effective Schools Products.

Long, N. J., Morse, W. C., Newman, R. G. (1980). *Conflict in the classroom*. Belmont, CA: Wadsworth Publishing Company.

Lyman, F. T. (1981). The responsive classroom discourse: The inclusion of all students. In A. Anderson (Ed.), *Mainstreaming digest* (109–113). College Park, MD: University of Maryland Press.

Martens, B. K. & Kelly, S. Q. (1993). A behavioral analysis of effective teaching. *School Psychology Quarterly, 8,* 10–26.

Martens, B. K., & Meller, P. J. (1990). The application of behavioral principles to educational settings. In T. B. Gutkin & C. R. Reynolds (Eds.), *The handbook of school psychology* (2nd ed.) (pp. 612–634). New York: John Wiley & Sons.

Marzano, R. J. (2001). In T. Scherer, How and why standards can improve student achievement: A conversation with Robert J. Marzano. *Educational Leadership, 59*(1), 14–18.

Marzano, R. J. (2003). *What works in schools: Translating research into action.* Alexandria, VA: Association for Supervision and Curriculum Development.

Marzano, R. J. (2006). *Classroom assessment and grading that work.* Alexandria, VA: Association for Supervision and Curriculum Development.

Marzano, R. J., & Pickering, D. J. (2005). *Building academic vocabulary: Teacher's manual.* Alexandria, VA: Association of Supervision and Curriculum Development.

Marzano, R. J., Pickering, D. J., & Pollock, J. E. (2001). *Classroom instruction that works: Research-based strategies for increasing student achievement.* Alexandria, VA: Association for Supervision and Curriculum Development.

Marzano, R. J., Waters, T., & McNulty, B. A. (2005). *School leadership that works: From research to results.* Alexandria, VA: Association for Supervision and Curriculum Development.

Mayer, G. R. (2000). *Classroom management: A California resource guide.* Los Angeles, CA: County Office of Education. Retrieved from http://wwwstatic.kern.org/gems/schcom/ClassroomManagement.pdf

Mayer, G. R., & Ybarra, W. J. (2004). *Teaching alternative behaviors schoolwide: A resource guide to prevent discipline problems.* Los Angeles, CA: County Office of Education. Retrieved from http://www.lacoe.edu/includes/templates/document_frame.cfm?toURL=/DocsForms/20031008084414_TABS.pdf

McEwan, E. K. (1998). *Seven steps to effective instructional leadership.* Thousand Oaks, CA: Corwin.

McNulty, B., & Besser, L. (2011). *Leaders make it happen! An administrator's guide to data teams.* Englewood, CO: Lead + Learn Press.

McTighe, J., & Wiggins, G. (2012). From common core standards to curriculum: Five big ideas. Available from http://grantwiggins.files.wordpress.com/2012/09/mctighe_wiggins_final_common_core_standards.pdf

Mercer, C. D., Campbell, K. U., Miller, D., Mercer, K. D., & Lane, H. B. (2000). Effects of a reading fluency intervention for middle schoolers with specific learning disabilities. *Learning Disabilities Research & Practice, 15*(4), 179–189.

National Commission on Excellence in Education. (1983). *A nation at risk: The imperative for educational reform.* Available from http://www2.ed.gov/pubs/NatAtRisk/risk.html

National Governors Association Center for Best Practices, & Council of Chief State School Officers. (2010a). *Common Core State Standards for English language arts & literacy in history/social studies, science, and technical subjects.* Washington, DC: Author. Available at www.corestandards.org/assets/CCSSI_ELA%20Standards.pdf

National Governors Association Center for Best Practices, & Council of Chief State School Officers. (2010b). *Common Core State Standards for mathematics.* Washington, DC: Author. Available at www.corestandards.org/assets/CCSSI_ELA%20Standards.pdf

National Institute of Child Health and Human Development. (2000). *Report of the National Reading Panel: Teaching children to read: An evidence-based assessment of the scientific research literature on reading and its implications for reading instruction: Reports of the subgroups* (NIH Publication No. 00–4754). Washington, DC: U.S. Government Printing Office.

National Mathematics Advisory Panel. (2008). *Foundations for success: The final report of the National Mathematics Advisory Panel.* Washington, DC: US Department of Education.

National Research Council. (2001). *Adding it up: Helping children learn mathematics.* Washington, DC: National Academy Press.

No Child Left Behind Act of 2001, Public Law 107–110, 5, 115 Stat. 1427 (2002), et seq.

Northeast Foundation for Children. (2013). *Responsive classroom.* Available at http:// www.responsiveclassroom.org.

Organisation for Economic Development and Co-Operation (OECD). (2011). *Lessons from PISA for the United States, strong performers and successful reformers in education.* OECD Publishing.

Pearson, P. D., & Gallagher, G. (1983). The gradual release of responsibility model of instruction. *Contemporary Educational Psychology, 8,* 112–123.

Peters, T. J., & Waterman, Jr., R. H. (1982). In *search of excellence: Lessons from America's best-run companies.* New York: HarperCollins.

Piaget, J. (1970). *Science of education and the psychology of the child.* New York: Orion Press.

Powell, S., & Nelson, B. (1997). Effects of choosing academic assignments on a student with attention deficit hyperactivity disorder. *Journal of Applied Behavior Analysis, 30,* 181–183.

Reason, C. (2010). *Leading a learning organization: The science of working with others.* Bloomington, IN: Solution Tree Press.

Reeves, D. B. (2002). *Making standards work: How to implement standards-based assessment in the classroom, school, and district.* Denver, CO: Advanced Learning Press.

Reeves, D. (2006). *The leading learner.* Alexandria, VA: Association for Supervision and Curriculum Development.

Reeves, D. B. (2009). Looking deeper into the data. *Educational Leadership, 66*(4), 89–90.

Scherer, M. (2001). How and why standards can improve student achievement: A conversation with Robert J. Marzano. *Making Standards Work, 59*(1), 14–18.

Schlechty, P. (1997). *Inventing better schools: An action plan for educational reform.* San Francisco: Jossey-Bass.

Schmoker, M. J. (2011) *Focus: Elevating the essentials to radically improve student learning.* Alexandria, VA: Association for Supervision and Curriculum Development.

Sprick, R. S., Borgmeier, C., & Nolet, V. (2002). Prevention and management of behavior problems in secondary schools. In M. A. Shinn, H. M. Walker, & G. Stoner (Eds.), *Interventions for academic and behavior problems II: Preventive and remedial approaches* (pp. 373–401). Bethesda, MD: National Association of School Psychologists.

Stanovich, K. E. (1986). Matthew effects in reading: Some consequences of individual differences in the acquisition of literacy. *Reading Research Quarterly, 21*(4), 360–407.

Stanovich, K. E. (1993). Does reading make you smarter? Literacy and the development of verbal intelligence. In Hayne W. Reese (Ed.), *Advances in Child Development and Behavior.* Oxford, UK: Elsevier Science.

Stiggins, R. J. (2007). Assessment for learning: An essential foundation of productive instruction. In D. Reeves (Ed.), *Ahead of the curve: The power of assessment to transform teaching and learning* (pp. 59–76). Bloomington, IN: Solution Tree Press.

Stiggins, R. & DuFour, R. (2009). Maximizing the power of formative assessments. *Phi Delta Kappan, 90*(9), 640–644.

Sugai, G., & Horner, R. (2002). The evolution of discipline practices: School-wide positive behavior supports. *Child & Family Behavior Therapy, 24,* 23–50.

Thompson, G. J., & Jenkins, J. B. (1993). *Verbal judo: The gentle art of persuasion.* New York: William Morrow.

U.S. Department of Education. (2004). *Teaching children with attention deficit hyperactivity disorder: Instructional strategies and practices.* Available at http://www.ed.gov/teachers/needs/speced/adhd/adhd-resource-pt2.doc

U.S. Department of Education. (2010). *National Center for Education Statistics, Digest of Education Statistics 2009* (NCES 2010–013). Washington, DC: U.S. Government Printing Office.

Valencia, S. W., & Buly, M. R. (2005). Behind test scores: What struggling readers really need. In S. J. Barrentine & S. M. Stokes (Eds.), *Reading assessment: Principles and practices for elementary teachers* (2nd ed.). Newark, DE: International Reading Association.

Vygotsky, L. S. (1978). *Mind and society: The development of higher mental processes.* Cambridge, MA: Harvard University Press.

Walker, H. M. (1997). *The acting-out child: Coping with classroom disruption.* Longmont, CO: SoprisWest.

Walker, H. M., Colvin, G., & Ramsey, E. (1995). *Antisocial behavior in school: Strategies and best practices.* Pacific Grove, CA: Brooks/Cole Publishing.

Walker, H. M., & Walker, J. E. (1991). *Coping with noncompliance in the classroom: A positive approach for teachers.* Austin, TX: Pro-Ed.

Webb, N. (1997). *Research Monograph Number 6: Criteria for alignment of expectations and assessments on mathematics and science education.* Washington, DC: The Council of Chief State School Officers.

Weber, C. (2013). *RTI in the early grades: Intervention strategies for mathematics, literacy, behavior & fine-motor challenges.* Bloomington, IN: Solution Tree Press.

Weiner, B. (2005). *Social motivation, justice, and the moral emotions: An attributional approach.* Mahwah, NJ: Lawrence Erlbaum Associates.

Wiggins, G. & McTighe, J. (2005). *Understanding by Design* (expanded 2nd ed.). Alexandria, VA: Association for Supervision and Curriculum Development.

Wiliam, D., & Thompson, M. (2007). Integrating assessment with instruction: What will it take to make it work? In C. A. Dwyer (Ed.), *The future of assessment: Shaping teaching and learning.* Mahwah, NJ: Lawrence Erlbaum Associates.

Wood, D., Bruner, J. S., & Ross, G. (1976). The role of tutoring and problem solving. *Journal of Child Psychology and Psychiatry, 17,* 89–100.

Wurman, Z., & Wilson, W. S. (2012). The common core math standards: Are they a step forward or backward? *Education Next, 12*(3).

Young, A. (2009). Using common assessments in uncommon courses. In T. R. Guskey (Ed.), *The teacher as assessment leader* (pp. 135–153). Bloomington, IN: Solution Tree Press.

Index

CORWIN
A SAGE Company

The Corwin logo—a raven striding across an open book—represents the union of courage and learning. Corwin is committed to improving education for all learners by publishing books and other professional development resources for those serving the field of PreK–12 education. By providing practical, hands-on materials, Corwin continues to carry out the promise of its motto: **"Helping Educators Do Their Work Better."**